ANOTHER B...
BORDE...

Also in Arrow by Lavinia Derwent

A BORDER BAIRN
A BREATH OF BORDER AIR
GOD BLESS THE BORDERS
A MOUSE IN THE MANSE

LAVINIA DERWENT

Another Breath of
Border Air

Illustrated by Elizabeth Haines

Arrow Books

Arrow Books Limited
62-65 Chandos Place, London WC2N 4NW

An imprint of Century Hutchinson Limited

London Melbourne Sydney Auckland
Johannesburg and agencies throughout
the world

First published by Hutchinson 1977
Arrow edition 1978
Reprinted 1980 and 1988

Printed and bound in Great Britain by
Anchor Brendon Limited, Tiptree, Essex

ISBN 0 09 917290 9

To Jessie – once more

Contents

1. Childhood in the Cheviots

When I was a child I could go abroad without a passport every single day if I liked. Across the Cheviot hills, over the Border and into that other country called England. Where the heathens lived, according to Jessie.

Jessie was my best friend. The others were mainly four-footed or feathered. Some were even wooden, like the tattie-bogles dotted around the fields to scare the crows, though I doubt if they ever did, for I often saw birds perching on the scarecrows' heads or pecking in their pockets for crumbs of comfort.

They gave me comfort, too, for they had time to stand still and listen, without assuming that grown-up air of always knowing best. The beasts, too, would lend an ear when I talked to them. Even Grumphy the pig turned his head and put on an interested expression when I had some news to impart.

'I was top of the class today and never got the strap once. Fancy that!'

Fancy that, indeed. Even if he only gave me a grunt in reply it was something.

Jessie would listen if she had time, but unlike the scarecrows she seldom stood still. If I wanted her attention I had to run after her from back kitchen to byre, or out into the fields if she was spreading dung or stooking corn. Jessie had a dual role, working in the house on some days and in the fields on others. But always working, never sitting still.

The men who worked on the farm were called hinds and the women bondagers. It was the height of my ambition to become a bondager when I grew up, but Jessie doubted if I had enough sense. Rummlegumption, she called it.

It was a world of its own, far from the main road and isolated from neighbours and passers-by. Everything revolved round the farmhouse where I lived. The Big Hoose, Jessie called it. She lived in a little house across the fields with her brother the shepherd and her sister Joo-anne who was a stay-at-home, except at busy times when she came out and worked as a bondager.

The hinds and their wives lived in the cottages down the road which I passed every morning on my way to school, and though the occupants of the herd's house never changed, the cottages sometimes had different curtains on the windows and new people at term time. But not often, for my father kept his workers year after year. It was an exciting event if a new hind and his family arrived. A chance to see some fresh faces, maybe some bairns to share my games.

I was an in-between, the third member of a growing family, less than the dust in the eyes of an elder brother and sister who were away getting their higher education. There was a young baby in the house taking up much of my mother's attention, so I had to make a life of my own. And I always had Jessie, strong and steady, the same yesterday, today, and for ever.

Out and about was the best place to be, with endless pleasures to pursue on the farm – even just swinging on a gate, though this was strictly forbidden. Gates were not toys. They were there for a practical purpose, to keep animals in the fields, and must never be left open.

'Shut that yett!' Jock-the-herd would shout at me. 'Man-lassie, are ye donnert?'

Being donnert meant having no common sense. No rummlegumption. We had a language of our own in the Borders, full of expressive words which I learnt from Jessie and the shepherd. I knew that if they called me a sumph it meant that I was stupid; but if they told me on rare occasions that I had smeddum, it was meant as a compliment. I had guts! But more often I was a sumph and swung on the gates whether it was forbidden or not.

It was a great feeling, sailing backwards and forwards, faster and faster, like flying through the air, until, of course, the inevitable happened. There came an ominous creak as one of the spars gave way, and then I was in real trouble. Jock would have to come with hammer and nails to patch up the damage, but, give him his due, though he told me my character, he never seemed to begrudge the time and trouble.

'Maybe ye'll lairn,' he would say hopefully. I did try, though not with much success. It would be wonderful to be grown-up and perfect. Or would it? Did Jessie never long to swing on a gate or turn somersaults? What a lot of fun I would miss when I was old and full of sense.

If I wanted to get away from everyone I took to my heels and went off to foreign parts. The best way was a short cut across the fields and braes instead of following the winding main road up to the Carter Bar. The coach road it was called in the days when the horse-driven mail-coaches came rattling over the twisting route from Newcastle to Edinburgh.

There, at the summit, I really was in the Borderland, one foot in one country and one in another, though I could see no sudden change in the landscape. An English tree looked much the same a Scottish one; Redesdale rabbits ran about on four legs, and there was heather growing on foreign soil.

The cows on the other side chewed thistles just as ours did, and a lark flew carelessly in the communal sky. The people, too, looked like ordinary human beings.

Only their tongues were different. They were Geordies and called me hinny instead of man-lassie as our shepherd did, but I could never see anything heathen about them. They were just people whose ancestors, true enough, had fought with ours in the old reiving days. But that was long ago and best forgotten.

The hills all had names. On the Northumberland side were Carterfell, Catcleuch Shin, Peel Fell, Hartshorn Pyke and many more, though I just lumped them all together as the Cheviots. I knew the Roxburghshire ones better, on our side: the Eildons, Ruberslaw, Minto Crags, the Dunion. But what did names matter? We had two of our own on the farm, which we just called the hill and the heathery hill and thought none the less of them.

I was convinced the Cheviots were in the Bible. Or, at least, in the psalm we sang at the kirk. 'I to the hills will lift mine eyes.' I often lifted mine to look at them and found them full of surprises, different every day. Sometimes with clouds scudding across their peaks, sometimes lost in a mist like a lady hiding behind her veil. At times they were far out of reach. On other days they seemed to have crept so close I could almost put out my hand and touch them.

> When Ruberslaw puts on his cowl,
> The Dunion on his hood,
> Then a' the wives o' Teviotdale
> Ken there will be a flood.

Jessie was an even better barometer. She could tell by the feeling in her bones when it was going to rain. No use washing blankets or starting the spring-cleaning if her big toe was 'stoonding'. There was sure to be a downpour.

Jessie never let on whether she liked me or not. It was different with her brother. I was sure of Jock-the-herd, but

I suppose he had nothing better to compare me with than one of his yowes. With Jessie around there was no chance of getting above myself. There was little I had to boast about, anyway, except that I had passed my Qualifying at the country school and was about to go to the Grammar School in Jedburgh, some eight miles away, to learn all sorts of strange subjects, including French.

'French!' scoffed Jessie. 'Ye'd mair need to lairn gumption.'

But that was not in the curriculum. Any I learned I got from Jessie herself. To this day I stop and think, 'Would *she* approve?', and if I still persist in disobeying my invisible mentor I have a feeling that she will 'give me my licks'.

I was well used to licks, especially from the teacher's tawse. Auld Baldy-Heid, the master at the village school, did not spare the rod. Once the leather strap was in his hand – the hangman's whip, we called it – he laid it on hard and fast, to boys and girls alike. We took it stoically enough and thought none the less of him. Indeed, deep down we had a great affection for the schoolmaster. One word of praise from him could send our spirits sky-high, and though his rage at times was fierce, he never actually carried out his constant threat to skin the lot of us alive.

Although I had now escaped from his clutches, Auld Baldy-Heid would always be the master to me, not just an ordinary man who sometimes came to visit my parents at the farmhouse. On such occasions I was on tenterhooks. 'Like a hen on a het girdle,' Jessie said. But how could I sit calmly beside him at the tea-table and pass the butter without trembling with terror? At any moment he might ask me to parse something or put his hand in his pocket and bring out the dreaded tawse.

If I was warned in time that he was coming I ran away and hid up a tree, or went off to my private haven, the broken-down Border Keep on the hill. This meant foregoing the special spread that had been laid on for his benefit, the sponge-cake oozing with fresh cream, the iced cake, the shortbread, the pancakes, and the variety of small scones, brown, plain and curranty. Not even the best strawberry jam would entice me. I could always eat scrogs – the wild crab-apples – or just starve. Better than being skinned alive.

Food, in any case, was not my priority. I preferred 'rubbish' – sweets, condensed milk, a sugar-piece, or any odds and ends I could cull from the hedgerows. Meals with a beginning, middle and end were a nuisance. It was a waste of time sitting in to the table and solemnly going through each course.

Yet, looking back, everything seemed to taste better in the old days. Floury potatoes, a feast in themselves, clooty-dumplings filled with juicy currants, roly-poly puddings, treacly gingerbread, barley-fadges, tasty ham from our own pig, occasional treats of succulent sausages bought from the butcher or kippers caught in far-off Loch Fyne.

Perhaps it was the long slow cooking over an open fire that gave the stews and stovies their extra flavour. Certainly we were never asked whether we liked anything or not. It was just served up to us, take it or leave it.

Town folk considered it a treat to drink warm frothy milk straight from the cow, but I preferred it after it had cooled in the dairy. The milk-hoose, we called the little room off the back-kitchen. Better still I liked the sharp taste of soor-dook, the buttermilk which was left after the churning. Beistie-pudding, made with beistie-milk, the first milking of a cow after she had calved, was thought to be the greatest delicacy. But not by me. I hated the sight and taste of it so much that I always tipped it into the pigs' pail rather than eat it.

'Mony a stervin' heathen wad be gled o't,' said Jessie; but I would sooner have starved.

I had been a passive observer often enough in the byre, where I sat on a small stool with a row of cats beside me waiting to be fed, but now Jessie decided it was time to teach me the art of milking for myself.

'It'll come in handier than French. Watch, lassie.'

I watched, but I would sooner have listened. Jessie had a great fund of stories, and though I had heard them over and over again I could never get enough of them. They were all about animals. Wee moudiwart, the mole, who lived under the ground, or the pig with the curly tail. Jessie had a great gift for words and told the stories so expressively in her rich dialect that I could see the furry creatures crawling under their earth-heaps or hear the curly-tailed pig crying for his mother when he was lost.

'Tell me a story, Jessie.'

'No, I'll no'. No' till ye've lairnt to milk.'

'A riddle, then. Please, Jessie.'

If I pleaded long enough she might give in. I knew all her riddles and their answers off by heart but I still liked to hear her recite them for she put on a different sing-song voice. The cats sat up on their tails and the cows turned their heads to watch her through their great solemn eyes when she began.

'Bonnie Kitty Brannie, she stands at the wa',
Gie her little, gie her muckle, she licks up a'.
Gie her stanes, she'll eat them – but waitter, she'll dee.
Can ye think o' an answer an' tell it to me?'

'Yes, I can, Jessie. It's a fire.'

'Ay, so it is, lassie;' but when I asked for another Jessie was not to be coaxed. 'Watch the milkin',' she said firmly. 'See hoo I strip the coo.'

Stripping was done gently but firmly at the end so that not a drop was wasted. I sat on my stool obediently watching, while the cats mieowed hungrily beside me and the bubbly-jock keeked in at the open door. The milk made a pleasant sound as it splashed into the pail. It looked easy enough, I thought.

During that first lesson we had company in the byre. A tramp woman who had been sheltering there for the night sat on the straw in a corner, itching to smoke her clay pipe but not daring to light it, for Jessie had given her a sharp warning about the danger of setting the place ablaze. She kept mumbling to herself and fingering a hidden pocket in the folds of her tattered skirt. If I had been alone with her, she could have smoked to her heart's content. But, then, I had no sense.

'Ye can begin wi' Bessie,' said Jessie, getting up from her stool. 'She's a quiet beast.'

Bessie, the brown cow, was not all that quiet. At the first go she gave me a skelp on the ear with her tail which sent me flying from the stool and brought stinging tears to my eyes.

'See!' said Jessie. 'It's no' that easy. There's a knack in't.'

So there was; one that took me ages to master. Bessie was none too pleased with my bungling attempts, nor was Jessie when the cow kicked over the pail and the milk went running in little rivulets across the byre floor with the cats lapping it up in hot pursuit.

The old crone drew out her empty pipe and sucked it for consolation like a baby with a dummy while Jessie gave me my character. The cats cowered, licking their milky mouths, and even the bubblyjock turned tail and fled. But there was no escape for me. I would not have my sorrows to seek, she warned me, unless I stuck in and made a better job of it.

So I did. Perseverance pays. After many a hard battle I mastered the art, even of stripping, and was prouder than having passed the Qualifying when Jessie gave me a pat on the back to show her approval.

'There noo, lassie! Ye can milk a coo, so ye're ready for onything. Ye'll never look back.'

But I do look back, often and often, and wish I could still be there in the byre with the cows whisking their tails and Jessie telling me one of her stories.

'A'weel, ance upon a time there was a wee weasel ca'd Wullie. . . .'

2. Freedom on the Farm

I learned a lot more during that long summer as I ran barefoot all over the farm, making the most of my freedom before plunging into the big world of the Grammar School.

Sometimes I spent the entire day in the old Border Keep, the ruined castle on the hill, queen of all I surveyed. I had no spy-glasses but there was plenty to observe with my own eyes, even just the sky itself which was always full of surprises. There were times when it seemed – like the hills – far out of reach, so high up that there was nothing there. On other days it was just above my head, with dark clouds bumping into each other as they scudded by. In sunny weather they were white and woolly, like newly clipped fleeces, or faintly tinged with pink from the rays of the sun. Heaven was up there amongst the clouds but I could never see it or hear any of the angels sing.

If I was lucky I would see a rainbow. Where was the pot of gold? I ran down the hill to the burn – the small Jed – to look for it, but tantalizingly it had changed its position.

Always the rainbow's ending was out of reach and there was no treasure to find, except an old boot bobbing about in the water or maybe a tattered umbrella.

From the look-out tower in the keep I could watch the comings and goings on the main road, not that there were many: the minister emerging from the manse gate with his little dog at his heels, the postie on his bicycle, the baker's horse and cart. Sometimes a more colourful sight, a gypsy caravan swaying on its way over the Border. Or perhaps 'the man with the stallion' walking the road on one of his mysterious missions. From time to time he came to our farm with his great prancing beast, and strange things took place round in the steading, but I was never allowed to be an onlooker.

Nearer at hand there was another road, moss-grown and rutted. The back road which was the driveway leading to Edgerston House where the laird lived. It was used by vans delivering goods to the Big House, and sometimes I saw a chauffeur-driven car gliding by with the laird himself sitting in the back.

He never noticed me, of course, though sometimes the chauffeur gave me a sideways smile. The laird was a higher being, akin to the Almighty, except that he did not give his all to the poor but gathered gear from his business enterprises in London where he spent most of his time. Yet he was kind enough to his estate-workers and sometimes, like God, he, too, could work miracles. When he visited the village school he made Auld Baldy-Heid give us a holiday.

Now that I think of it the laird had a look of the Good Shepherd about him when he arrived at the school with a cloak draped over his shoulders and a long stick in his hand like Jock's crook. We all sat up straight and hoped he would not speak to us for we could never understand a word he said. He spoke English, we presumed, but not plain enough for us to comprehend, and we were never sure whether to say 'Eh?' or 'Beg pardon' when he asked us a question.

Doubtless he was equally bamboozled by our replies. I remember one day he paused at Big Bob's desk. The laddie was chewing his pencil at the time and trying his best to look invisible.

'And what are you doing, boy?' asked the laird in his clipped tongue.

Big Bob looked up at him like a startled rabbit.

'Eh? Beg pardon'

The laird repeated his question a little louder and a little faster. 'I said what are you doing, boy?'

Big Bob got the message at last and answered literally, 'I'm chowin' ma pencil.'

'Oh,' said the laird, looking puzzled. 'Well, carry on, boy.'

So Big Bob took him at his word and carried on chewing his pencil.

The only time the laird stopped at my desk he asked the customary daft question older people so often put to children.

'And what are you going to be when you grow up, little girl?'

My answer was brief and to the point. 'Big.' I added 'sir' when I saw Auld Baldy-Heid glowering at me, but I was not being cheeky, just truthful like Big Bob.

Strangely enough we had no difficulty in understanding the laird when he announced, 'I have asked the teacher to give you a half-holiday and he has agreed. Does that suit you, children?'

'Yessir!'

We cheered him to the echo and he went away with his cloak flapping behind him, feeling no doubt that he had done his duty nobly. And so he had. We were out of the classroom like bumbees from a byke before the master could change his mind.

Having a half-holiday did not mean getting home any earlier. Often the opposite. With all the time in the world at our disposal there were a hundred pleasant ploys we could pursue. We could indulge in a rowdy game of kick-the-can in the playground before dawdling down the road, hitting out at each other with our schoolbags or climbing fences to play hide-and-seek in the woods.

I cannot recall feeling tired or hungry in those far-off days. Or even wet, though surely it must have poured with rain many a time. Not that a drenching would have dampened our spirits. If we were engrossed in some pursuit we just went on and on, with no grown-up to stop our fun.

Often it would be dark by the time I arrived home, with holes in my stockings, my hair in a tangle, and the buttons torn off my coat.

'Sic a slaister ye're in,' Jessie would say severely. (A slaister meant a mess.) 'What kept ye so late?'

'I got a half-holiday,' I told her, and that was explanation enough.

But now that I had left the village school I had whole holidays every day and never any problem about how to fill the long hours. Sometimes I went and lay in the meadow – the cow-gang – rich with gowans, grasses and myriads of wild flowers all mingled together. They had a heady perfume which attracted the bees and butterflies, and I lay in a drowsy haze of scent and sound, feeling slightly tipsy. The cows nibbled at my bare toes and Flora, the white pony, came cantering from the other end of the field to crop the grass near by. I felt as if I belonged to the earth and was part of everything that grew around me.

When I heard the shepherd shouting to Jed and Jess I came to life. According to Jessie I was a peerie-top and liked to be on the go. And it was not all play, for I took my turn at helping in the fields, fancying myself as a fully-fledged bondager. Without me the hay would never have got cut or the corn stooked. It was a puzzle how they managed when I was away at the school.

Mine, in truth, were the most menial tasks, fetching and

carrying for the hinds or holding the horses' heads, if I could reach up to them. I was not at ease with the Clydesdales when they showed their strong teeth. Were they smiling at me or sneering? Sometimes they reached down with a jangle of harness and tore out great mouthfuls of grass from the ground. They would eat anything, even a piece of sticky toffee if I offered it to them on my palm, but I was always afraid they might swallow my hand as well.

Turning the hay was a simple enough task except that the giant forks used by the farm-workers were too cumbersome for me to manipulate. So I did the job with my hands, which were soon stinging with thistles. Thristles, Jessie called them. She would gouge them out of my thumbs with a darning-needle, putting on her spectacles for the purpose. Communal glasses they were, for I sometimes saw her sister, Joo-anne, wearing them as she sat by the fire in the herd's house, turning the heel of a sock; and I think Jock wore them too when he was looking up Deuteronomy in the kirk.

The men never seemed to get thristles, nor Jessie. Perhaps she wore leather gloves, though I doubt it. Her hands were as hard as iron except on washing-days, when her fingers were covered with soft ridges after rubbing the clothes for so long on the scrubbing-board. On Sundays she certainly wore gloves when she went to church, and blew into them when she took them off and laid them neatly on the ledge in her pew.

When the hay had been raked into little ricks and left long enough to winnow, the great day came when it was ready to be carted in from the fields and built into haystacks.

Weather was the important factor, and it was my father, the Boss, who decided when the operation should begin. I often wondered if he had a direct line with God, for he looked skywards so often before passing on word to the workers. Father was never an orderer, only a suggester, and the hinds seemed to respect him all the more for this seeming lack of authority.

'The weather looks right. Maybe we should make a start.'

It was all hands to work. The herd came in from the hirsel, Jessie abandoned her household tasks, and Joo-anne joined us, wearing her big bondager's hat. The men dragged out the wooden bogey from the cartshed and yoked in one of the horses, while the cocks and hens who had been using it as a roosting-place flew off with indignant protests, leaving a trail of fluff and feathers behind.

As soon as Tam shouted 'Gee-up!' and the bogey began to move, I jumped on for my first ride out to the hayfield.

> Rattle his bones over the stones,
> He's only a pauper whom nobody owns.

One of the men used to quote this to me. Tam or Wull. True enough the bogey was an uncomfortable mode of transport. It creaked and shook as it rumbled on its way, and I was always in danger of sliding off, especially when it stuck going through a gate.

'We'll need to get that yett aff,' the men would shout, then Jock-the-herd would have to come to the rescue to take it off its hinges. Nothing ever stumped him, making or mending. He always had nails in his pocket and a ready hand with a hammer.

The bogey came and went with its load, swaying into the stackyard where the neat pyramids of hay began to mount up into a small forest, later to be thatched and held in place with straw ropes. There was an art in building the haystacks from the base upwards, not too tightly packed for fear they would steam and go on fire. No amateur was allowed to do the job, though that was the height of my ambition, to prance about on the stack, fashioning it into the right shape.

It took an expert like Jessie, helped sometimes by the

Boss himself. They stood there at the receiving end, gathering the great forkfuls of hay into their arms and placing them in positions which looked higgledy-piggledy at first glance but which always miraculously ended in the right pattern.

The higher the stacks grew the harder it was for the men to fork up the hay from the bogey. Often the sweat broke on their brows, and they must have been thankful to rest their aching arms when I was sent running to the farmhouse to bring out the tea.

I liked when they let me climb the ladder propped against the haystack so that I could hand the tea and scones to Jessie and my father. The men had a quick draw at their pipes, then they were up and at it again, making the most of daylight and good weather while it lasted.

It was often pitch dark before they brought in the last load, and not a grumble from any of them about overtime. If the going was good it never occurred to any of us to stop. Often I was half asleep and the owls were hooting before I took my last bumpy ride on the bogey. My hair was full of hayseeds, and my legs covered with scratches. And even though I was only one of the lower orders, I had a feeling of achievement every time I went into the yard and saw the sturdy stacks standing there. I had helped in some small degree to build them.

There was even more hustle and bustle at harvest-time. I liked watching the whirring flails of the reaper going round and round, cutting the corn till there was only one small patch left in the middle of the field, the last refuge for the wild creatures who had been lurking amongst the corn. Rabbits, hares, mice, hedgehogs and lame birds had retreated out of the way of the relentless reaper and were now huddled together, strange bedfellows, awaiting their fate.

> Wee sleekit, cow'rin tim'rous beastie,
> O what a panic's in thy breistie!

Their fate was sealed when the herd whistled up his dogs and the hinds advanced on the corn patch shouting and brandishing sticks. I turned my head away from the slaughter and was always glad when a scurrying rabbit darted through the men's legs and went bobtailing away to safety.

That night everyone went home with a share of the spoil, and, in spite of my squeamishness, I enjoyed the rabbit pie or hare soup as well as any. Somehow, now that the beasties had lost their identity I could only spare them a passing pitying thought while relishing their savoury taste.

Though we used Shanks' pony a great deal in the country, we never just went for a walk. There was always a purpose behind it.

I walked the two miles to school, of course, and two miles back, then sometimes at night I was sent to shut in the hens. This meant another long trudge to distant parts of the farm where the henhouses were dotted around. And, since hens were not early-bedders, it meant going in that eerie half-darkness of the gloaming when there were strange rustlings to be heard and bogles seemed to be lurking behind every tree.

Fashious creatures, Jessie called the hens, and so they were. The last thing they wanted was to be shut in for the night. Yet I had to make sure that every one of them entered the wee trapdoor, for there were foxes prowling around and I would get what for if any of the Black Minorcas or Rhode Island Reds were missing in the morning.

The hens tried every trick to elude me. I pleaded, threatened, and chased after them in a desperate game of hide-and-seek. They seemed to be laughing up their feathers at me, but at length I always captured the lot. What a relief when every trapdoor was finally shut and my task was over.

Not quite over, for I had been told by Jessie, 'Never come hame empty-handed. Aye pick up a wheen sticks to bring back.'

So I used to gather odds and ends of firewood as I wended my way home. Some were large branches so unwieldy that I had to drag them behind me and often dropped more than I picked up, especially when I had to open gates or climb fences. But I always came home with something even if it was only a handful of fir cones. They gave out a fine fragrance when flung on the fire. I liked to hear them sizzling and watch their changing colours.

I never met a bogle on those evening walks, but sometimes I came face to face with the herd who was much more comforting and helped me over dykes with my burdens. He also offered me some sound advice.

'Man-lassie, can ye no' cairry the sticks ablow your oxter?' Under my arm, he meant.

The trouble was, my oxter was not as strong as Jock's. Try as I would, I always left a trail behind me and was for ever having to turn on my tracks to pick up the fallen.

Sometimes, in the dim light, I picked up more than I expected. One night I took hold of a prickly hedgehog by mistake thinking he was a lump of wood. On another occasion it was a small black kitten who had come creeping after me in the darkness. No wonder I was always glad when I could see the glow of the lamplit kitchen window.

I remember one murky night I saw something white moving towards me. A ghost. What else? Too petrified to turn and flee, I stood stock still letting my load of sticks fall to the ground. The next moment the ghost spoke to me in Jessie's familiar voice.

'Where the dickens hae ye been, lassie?' she said, advancing towards me wearing a long white apron over her black skirt. 'I thought ye'd gane an' got lost. An' you empty-handed, tae! I've tell't ye afore, ye should never come hame withoot something under your oxter.'

3. The Back of Beyond

As well as owning our own farm, Overton Bush, my father rented another in the Oxnam district some six or seven miles away in the wilds. A hill farm called Swinside Townhead. From a duke, no less. The Duke of Roxburghe who lived in an enormous mansion like Buckingham Palace: Floors Castle at Kelso.

I never set eyes on the duke who was an even higher personage than the laird, but once a year my father and the other tenants were bidden to a gathering at Kelso where they lunched with His Grace and ceremoniously handed over their rents.

In real money, I think; for I can remember Father with a bag of golden sovereigns which he kept locked in his safe. They were not my kind of money, of course, like the homely halfpennies I spent at Bella Confectionery's shop, but it would have been fun, I felt, to play with such clean clinking coins.

I used to picture the duke sitting before a great heap of

shining sovereigns, like the king in his counting-house, letting them run through his fingers and gathering up more as each farmer came forward and showered down his offering.

When Father came home he always had great tales to tell, for he was a fine raconteur, of what the duke had said and done, but I was disappointed to hear that His Grace behaved like an ordinary mortal, eating steak-pie with the rest, and that the knives and forks were not of solid gold.

The hill farm, Swinside Townhead, seemed to be run by remote control. Except that once a week Father yoked Flora or Ginger into the gig and drove away to see what was what. My mother often accompanied him, and on rarer occasions I was allowed to go, sitting back-to-back with my parents and always in danger of tumbling out into the ditch.

At our farm road-end, instead of turning left as I did when going to school, Father tugged the pony's head to the right and the gig wheels went spinning away into less familiar territory towards Oxnam. Ousenam was the old word for it, and the river was called Ousenam Water. We were great ones in the Borders for double-naming. Swinside Townhead, to which we were aiming, was often called Soonside Toonheid. Little wonder we puzzled the foreigners from the other side.

They had been here, the Sassenachs, in the old feuding days, creeping across to pillage our farms while we were creeping in the opposite direction to steal their cattle; and they had left many a mark behind them. One of the farms we passed by was called Bloodylaws. 'For three days,' said an old account of the massacre, 'it had been running with blood.' I always expected Ousenam Water to look like the Red Sea, but it went purling on its way as pure as our own small burn at home.

There was not much traffic on the side roads apart from the odd tinker or mugger driving their lean half-starved horses. I was never sure which were muggers and which tinkers. The muggers had originally made earthenware mugs and hawked them round the countryside, but now both tinks and muggers appeared to specialize in pots and pails, and in mooching what they could get at each cottage door.

They had the reputation of being tarry-fingered and were different from the gypsies, less romantic, more scruffy, with tangled hair and wild looks in their eyes. They did not wheedle, they demanded, pushing their way into houses and helping themselves to any scraps they could find lying about. Yet they were skilled workmen when it came to soldering pots and pans, sharpening scissors or mending broken implements. For all that, they were not welcome guests. They were God's creatures, of course, but according to Jessie, 'He must hae made them on ane o' His aff-days.'

When we came near to Swinside there always seemed to be a look-out laddie at the turn of the road who ran helter-skelter into the farmhouse to give the warning that the Boss had arrived. The grieve who acted as factor in my father's absence lived there with his family, and always seemed to be leaning on something. Against the door, on a spade or a chair, never actually doing anything except chewing his droopy moustache.

Everything about the grieve was droopy. His trousers, his buttonless shirt, his braces which he held on to and twanged now and again, his left eye which looked in a different direction from his right. And his wife, the Missis.

The Missis was a dim, colourless, apologetic creature. Indeed she had a great deal to be apologetic about. Even I could sense the general air of discomfort and see how fushionless she was, with her down-at-heel slippers, her skirt fastened with a safety-pin and her lank locks coming adrift from their hairpins. The draughty kitchen was always in a state of chaos – dirty dishes on the table, ashes strewn in the fireplace, unwashed clothes scattered untidily on the chairs, cocks and hens wandering in through the open door. There was always a bairn, who would have been the better of a handkie, tugging at his mother's torn skirt.

While my father and the grieve went off to look around the farm, the Missis put on the kettle and dusted a chair for my mother to sit on. Then she started her apologizing.

'We're a bit behind hand this morning. The bairn was teething in the night.' Or the cow was calving. Or Himself, her husband, had been working late. A likely story!

I never waited for the tea out of the cracked cups served with slices of dubious seed-cake, but went off on my own up to the cottages where the Swinside hinds lived. They were all strangers to me, for unlike those on our own farm they seldom stayed more than a year. At term time my father was for ever having to hire new ones. They liked the place, and the Boss all right, but maybe it was the grieve who was the problem. My mother often urged Father to give the man the sack, but the Boss was too soft-hearted. 'Where could he go with all those bairns? Nobody would hire him.' So the farm suffered.

My objective during those visits was the Back of Beyond, past the cottage gardens on the brow of the hill where the wind whipped the washing on the clothes lines and bent the stunted gooseberry bushes to the ground. There was one gean tree – a wild cherry – which seldom bore fruit. The delicate blossom no sooner appeared than it was blown away; and so was I if I did not plant my feet firmly enough on the ground.

It was a strange feeling leaning against the wind, walking and yet standing still. Past the cottages there was nothing but a bumpy road leading away to the hills. The Back of Beyond. It was a breathless sight in more ways than one, this unfamiliar view of the Cheviots, fold upon fold all merging into each other. Even the birds that winged overhead seemed wilder, giving out strange calls as they skimmed off into the unknown.

There were farmsteads out there even more isolated than our own. I remember driving with my parents to visit the folk living in a house lurking near a wood at the foothills. I had to jump down from the back of the gig to open the rickety gates across the road, and wait to shut them again when the pony had cantered through. It was a tiresome task, getting off and on, and manipulating the awkward fastenings. Some were tied with binder-twine, others had home-made hooks that took me all my time to unlatch; and though we were sure of a warm welcome and a splendid tea when we arrived, I wondered if it was worth it. There was always the journey back and those awful gates to face. There was the dread, too, when it grew dark that the gig would drive away without me and I would be left in the wilds to perish, like Lucy Gray.

Even in daylight I did not linger long in the Back of Beyond, long enough, though, for the scene to be firmly implanted in my mind, so that today I have only to close my eyes and I can see that bleak landscape and hear the whaups calling in the blustery sky.

I had to keep on the alert for I was never sure when my parents would be ready to drive back home. Sometimes I saw Father and the grieve wandering round the fields or talking to the hinds. When they made their way towards the farmhouse I ran back to the kitchen where the Missis was still whining as she packed some eggs into a battered basket. We had plenty of eggs at Overton Bush but these were to sell to the vanman when he called at our door, as a nest-egg for my mother's private purse. But not before they had been cleaned and sorted out. The grieve's wife apologized for the shells being dirty and some of the eggs cracked. She had had no time to get them ready. There had been the calves to feed and the cows to milk, and she had had to send for the doctor last night for wee Mary who had come out in a rash. Ringworm. Caught from the pig. The bairn *would* wander into the stye. Then there had been the chimney smoking and the roof leaking.

I never listened, the story was too familiar. It was a relief to get away with the entire family waving us off and Himself leaning against the garden gate, his eyes looking in opposite directions. I could hear my father and mother discussing the unsatisfactory situation as I sat with my back to them in the gig, guarding the eggs.

They never brought me into the conversation. What would I know about anything? I could not even be trusted to look after the eggs properly, for on one dreadful occasion Ginger stumbled going downhill, jolting me out of the gig, and the basket came flying after me. I did try to catch it before it came crashing down beside me on the road, but it was no use. The next moment I was surrounded by egg-yolks and broken shells, and somehow it was all my fault. Solitary confinement in the garret would be my punishment when I got home.

Though I enjoyed my drives in the gig I longed for transport of my own. There was always a niggle of worry in my mind. How was I going to travel every day to the big school in Jedburgh when the time came? My elder brother had ridden there and back on Flora, but I could not see myself staying in the saddle long enough, far less getting on the pony's back in the first place, even with the aid of the mounting-stone at the kitchen door. The loupin'-on stane, Jessie called it. And who would hoist me up for the return journey?

The solution to my mind, was a bicycle. I had always hankered after one, and for years had pleaded with my parents, and with Santa Claus, to bring me one, but they were all deaf to my pleas. So I had to content myself with a broken-down machine which had long lain in the scrap-heap. The baneshaker, the herd called it, and he was not wrong.

I was no mechanic myself, but when I begged Jock to

help me, he put it into some sort of shape. At least he straightened the handlebars, tied them up with string and fixed the loose pedals. There were still some spokes missing, the tyres were punctured and the brakes unreliable. But the bell was perfect.

The biggest drawback to the baneshaker was its sex. It was a man's bicycle with a high spar which I could never manage to negotiate, so I had to ride sideways with one leg under the spar, a perilous way to pedal and no mean feat, now that I come to look back on it. In later years, when I came to grips with a real bicycle, I had a long tussle before I could ride it in a straightforward manner.

'Man-lassie, that contraption'll be the daith o' ye,' the herd used to warn me, and sure enough the baneshaker did its best. Many a time I went crashing into a wall or landed in the ditch with the baneshaker on top of me, but its erratic behaviour was all part of the fun.

I did not venture far, of course, but only around the farmyard, ringing the bell to scatter the livestock out of the way and occasionally coming to grief if the sow suddenly crossed my path. I realized I could never get as far as the Grammar School on such a broken-down charger. Once and once only I ventured out on to the main road. It was nearly the end of me as well as the bicycle.

I had been told to go to Bella's shop at Camptown about a mile away to get some bath-brick which the servant-girl used when scouring knives. In a fit of bravado I decided to go on the bicycle, but only as far as the road-end.

I set off riding sideways as usual. It was a rough journey down the bumpy road and I took many a toss. Once I fell into a clump of nettles and had to rub docken leaves on my hands and legs to take away the sting. No sooner was I remounted than I was off again, into a whin bush this time, but I was used to such mishaps and so was the bike. I had meant to leave it propped against a tree at the foot of the road, but as I was nearing the road-end the brakes refused to work. It was downhill and I was gathering speed all the time, so there was nothing for it but to turn left and continue my wobbly ride on the main road.

It was the first time I had ridden on such a smooth surface, and I had no idea the baneshaker could go at such a speed. I clung on, trying my best to keep a straight furrow and praying that no one would stray across my path. There were no cocks, pigs or bubblyjocks here. Worse, there were motor cars and lorries swerving past and a tinker's cart in front.

I rang my bell in desperation but the tink did not hear me. By now the baneshaker was out of control and all I could do was close my eyes when it ran slap-bang into the back of the cart. For a moment I saw stars, and the next thing I knew I was lying on the roadside with the tinker's pony cropping the grass beside me.

It was the end of the baneshaker for a time. The tink tried to make a bargain with me. He could use the remains of the bike as scrap if I liked to swap it for one of his pots or kettles. But, bleeding nose and all, I stuck to my guns and refused. When he had gone, I hid the broken bicycle in the ditch and struggled on to Bella Confectionery's to buy the bath-brick.

'Ye're a sorry sicht,' she told me, and lent me a red-and-white spotted handkerchief to stem the blood. She also gave me a piece of her home-made toffee which helped to soothe my wounded spirits.

Later, I persuaded Jock-the-herd to rescue the baneshaker's remains. He carried it home over his shoulder, protesting, 'Man-lassie, I doot it's had it this time.' But, 'Oh no,' I protested, 'the bell still rings.'

Once more he patched it up and I was able to pedal round the farmyard again. It was my plaything for years, and finally ended up on the rockery with all kinds of greenery growing over it. Perhaps it is there yet, and if so the bell will still be working.

It would be about this time that I saw my first aeroplane. It was when I was alone in the keep on the hill. A sudden shower had come on and I was sheltering in the great stone fireplace when I heard the throbbing in the sky as if a hundred motor cars were riding overhead. At first I thought it was the end of the world. The sky would split and a host of angels, or maybe devils, would come down and fetch me away.

I remember cowering down and trying to pray, but all I could think of was one of my father's comic songs. 'There was a wee cooper wha' lived in Fife. Nickety, nackety, noo-noo-noo!' So I settled for that instead.

It had no effect on the monster in the sky. The throbbing grew louder and louder till the giant seemed to be hovering immediately above my head. I looked up in terror through the open chimney-place, and there it was, a great mechanical bird, flying away through the mist in the direction of the Carter Bar. Mystified, I went out into the rain and watched it till it vanished over the Border. Then there was nothing. I waited for ages to see if it would come back, but it never did.

4. Gilding the Lily

It is an old Scottish characteristic that we see the faults in other people and never notice our own. When the minister preached on Sunday from the text, 'Judge not that ye be not judged,' I had a feeling he was aiming at me. I was for ever trying to put folk right, but seldom succeeding.

The servant-lasses, for example. We had a succession of these gawky creatures whom Jessie tried to lick into shape as if breaking in wild animals, but they never came up to her high standards. Poor things, they must have had a hard time, sent to work the moment they left school, longing to go out and play instead of washing up endless dishes, scrubbing the kitchen floor and blacking the fireplace.

Some stayed in, others tramped across the hills from neighbouring farms where their fathers were hinds or shepherds, and trudged back again at night when their work was done. I remember their hands, red and rough, sometimes covered with hacks and chilblains in winter. One I used to see blubbering into the kitchen sink. My heart bleeds for her; too late.

Liz-Ann is the one I remember best. She had been one of the big girls at school when I was an infant. Not very bright, according to the master, but he said the same about us all. Certainly she got the strap more often than the rest of us and used to sit on her hands afterwards, staring blankly at the blackboard.

Mental arithmetic was her downfall. Mine, too. How could one keep all those figures in the head and add them up, especially if one of the big boys was trying to put us 'off the stot' by tugging at our hair or thrusting inky blotting-paper down the backs of our necks? Poor Liz-Ann got lost right from the start. Her answer was always, 'I dinna ken.' Even with a pencil and jotter she never got as far as fractions.

Her efforts at writing essays were even more disastrous. The cruel thing, far more wounding than the strap, was that Auld Baldy-Heid sometimes read them out for all the class to giggle over. The spelling, too, must have been terrible, but we never saw that, only heard the master's sarcastic tones as he read out Liz-Ann's latest gem.

'Listen to this,' he would begin in a gloating voice. '"My holiday. I have not had no holiday. Was once at m'Auntie's in Hawick. Just for the day. Nice. Seen shops, got a new ribbing for my hair, blue. M'Auntie's got a bad leg."' And so on.

Maybe it was funny, but I used to glower at Auld Baldy-Heid, hating him as he read the smudged writing, and pitying poor Liz-Ann with her reddened shamed face. Judge not that ye be not judged.

When she turned up in our kitchen I determined to be nice to her and shield her, if I could, from Jessie's wrath, but soon I was seeing her faults myself. Everything Liz-Ann touched seemed to come away in her hand. She burnt the potatoes, knocked over pans, broke bowls, dropped bags of meal on the floor and fell over the cat. She was such a clumsy clattering creature that Jessie christened her the Cairthorse.

She lived in, and sometimes I had to share her bed if visitors were staying the night. Her room was small with a skylight, and no space for a human being to turn round in, far less a carthorse. I was surprised to see how Liz-Ann climbed into bed in her long goonie, lay down and went instantly to sleep, as if she had died. I never did. I had to stay awake for ages, sorting out all the things in my head and thinking over everything that had happened that day.

It seemed that I had no sooner fallen asleep than the alarum rang with a harsh ugly sound. It roused me immediately, but not the Cairthorse who only grunted and dived deeper under the bedclothes. By this time I was hanging half out of the bed, for it was narrow enough to begin with and Liz-Ann seemed to have expanded in all directions during the night. Often I had to shake the poor creature awake, and she rose in a heap, her face crumpled and her eyes still half-shut.

She lit the candle and dressed like a whirlwind in the freezing darkness of the dawn, pulling on one unshapely garment after another, and finally tying herself into an enveloping apron.

I felt it unfair that I should lie on, in the warm nest she had left, while she trailed away downstairs to her tasks, and had half-hearted thoughts of getting up to lend her a hand, but I never did. Instead, I fell into a blissful sleep in the great hollow left by Liz-Ann, with the patchwork quilt all to myself, and did not wake till the sun came streaming in through the skylight window.

Goodness knows how many dreary jobs the Cairthorse had done by the time I went down into the kitchen, ready for my breakfast. She had lit the fire, swept the floor, stirred the porridge, carried in sticks, scrubbed the table, peeled the potatoes. And doubtless broken the teapot.

What did Liz-Ann do in her spare time? I remember her

sitting dejectedly at the kitchen table, leaning on her elbows and staring into space, or turning over the pages of the sheep-dip catalogue. Sometimes I tried to cheer her up by playing the wheezy gramophone and getting her to hop round the kitchen with me, but she could never keep in time to the tune and only tramped on my toes. In her stocking-soles, fortunately, not in her clogs.

Now and again she came out to play hide-and-seek, but even at that the Cairthorse had no skill. I could crouch behind the water barrel, keep as still as a mouse, and never be seen. Not Liz-Ann, who blundered about like a bullock and always gave herself away by her heavy breathing.

On her day off she went clumping away home and had little to say when she came back with a bundle of clean clothing under her arm, tied in brown paper.

'How did you get on, Liz-Ann?'

'Fine.'

One day I discovered that the Cairthorse was not as dumb as she looked. She had a secret. I found out about it when she was struggling to write a letter at the kitchen table, and making heavy weather of it, sighing, sucking her pencil and staring at the ceiling for inspiration.

She tried to shield it from me, then in despair she asked, 'How d'ye spell crossroads?'

'Crossroads?' said I, not very sure myself. 'Who are you writing to?'

Liz-Ann turned as red as raspberry jam and looked over her shoulder to see that no one was listening. Then, with a faint touch of pride in her voice, she confessed: 'I'm writin' to ma lad.'

'Mercy me!'

I stared at her, dumbfounded. I knew it was every servant-girl's ambition to 'get a lad' and eventually a wedding-ring. It was their only escape from service, though it seemed to me they were only exchanging one set of shackles for another. But it had never occurred to me that the ungainly Cairthorse could ever attract a follower. Yet here she was sweating over a letter to her lad.

His name, she told me, was George (though I saw she had spelt it Gorge, which was near enough, I suppose). A herd-laddie, he lived somewhere in the region of the Back of Beyond and sometimes met Liz-Ann on her day off. That was as far as it had gone, but it was enough to put a sparkle in her eye when she spoke his name. He was a lad, and the Cairthorse was not going to let him slip through her fingers, clumsy though they were.

In the end she handed over the letter to me and I finished it off as well as I could. If Auld Baldy-Heid had seen it, with its crossings-out and misspellings, he would certainly have given Liz-Ann the strap, and me, too; but at least it was short and to the point.

The burden of it was 'Dear Gorge, will meet you at the crossroads on Sunday at six. Yours truly, Liz-Ann.'

'Would you not like to put with love, Liz-Ann?' I suggested.

'Oh no! What wad he think?'

I never met Gorge, but I saw him once wheeling his bicycle near the crossroads, with Liz-Ann striding along a few paces behind him, like a shaggy sheep-dog. He was only a wee fellow with tousled hair and tackety boots, but he was better then nothing. I often wonder if Liz-Ann married him and had lots of little carthorses. Perhaps she and Gorge spent their honeymoon at M'Auntie's in Hawick.

I remember that in anticipation of the wedding (if there was to be one) I made an attempt to save up to buy something for her bottom drawer. At that time I kept my riches in a china pig on a shelf in the kitchen. A thrifty, Jessie called it. It reminded me of the ditty she sometimes sang in the byre when milking the cows, about Coltart who made a special kind of candy, flavoured with aniseed, and travelled in the Borders selling it.

Allabally, Allabally bee,
Sittin' on your mammie's knee,
Greetin' for another bawbee
To buy some Coltart's candy.

Mither, gie's ma thrifty doon
Coltart's comin' to the toon,
Wi' a feather in his croon,
To sell some Coltart's candy.

There was never much money in my thrifty so I used to
put in a few buttons and safety-pins to make it rattle a bit
more. I found a small key and popped that in as well, never
thinking it had a vital use.

The day came, of course, when everyone was hunting
high and low for it.

'Ye've no' swallowed it?' asked Jessie, looking at me
suspiciously. 'The key to your faither's hat box. He's gaun
to a funeral an' he canna get oot his lum hat.'

'What's it like?' I asked guiltily.

'The lum hat? Toots! ye ken fine what a lum hat looks
like. It's got a high heid. . . .'

'No, no. The key. Was it a wee small one?'

'Ay, it was a wee sma' ane,' said Jessie, grabbing me by
the scruff of the neck. 'Whaur is't?'

'It's in the pig,' I had to confess.

'Ye're a daft eediot,' said Jessie angrily. 'Come on, get it
oot.'

The trouble with the thrifty was, though it was easy
enough putting things it, it was not so easy getting them
out. It took the entire family working with bread-knives
and scissors to disgorge its contents. A farthing here, a halfpenny there, a button, a back-stud, a darning-needle. Finally
the missing key, but by that time my father had been
forced to go hatless to the funeral.

'Noo, see here,' said Jessie, beginning to read me one of

her lessons, 'there's naething to gang into that thrifty but siller. D'ye hear me? Naething.'

Suitably chastened, I put back the few coins and replaced the pig on the shelf. I used to rattle it now and again in the hope that its contents had multiplied by magic, but they never did. Sometimes the herd or the postie, or even an Ingan Johnny who came in for a cup of tea, added the odd halfpenny, but my savings seldom grew beyond sixpence, so there was little hope of buying anything for Liz-Ann's 'doon-sittin'', apart from maybe a duster. Then one day the cat knocked the thrifty off the shelf and smashed it to smithereens. So that was the end of the pig.

In my efforts to be helpful to the Cairthorse I suggested she should curl her hair with the tongs to improve its lankness. The 'tings', Jessie called them. But Liz-Ann made a mess of that, too, by burning her brow and looking a worse sight than ever.

Who was I to speak? My hair was always 'toozy', and the only treatment it received was getting the ends singed once a week. A perfect pest. It was Jessie who did the deed, and I was always in terror lest she set my whole head on fire.

'An' so I wull, if ye dinna sit still.'

Singeing the hair was supposed to make it grow thicker. 'Though your heid's thick enough already, an' no' muckle intil't.'

Jock-the-herd was as bald as a billiard ball, not that he was often seen without a hat, except in the kirk. He seemed so self-conscious about his bare head that he kept taking out a large handkerchief and rubbing it over his pate, till Jessie dug him in the ribs and gave him one of her glowers.

I once asked her, 'Did you never singe Jock's hair?'

'No, I never. It's only lasses.'

So I tried it on a doll with a mop of bright flossy hair (but that was before I passed my Qualifying and learnt a modicum of sense). The results were disastrous. Flames shot all over the poor creature's head, her waxen face began to melt, and Jessie had to plunge her hastily into a pail of water. She was never the same again.

Though the herd would never have dreamt of beautifying himself, he sometimes tried to improve the looks of his flock before taking them to the sales. 'Toshing them up', he called it. He even dabbed a kind of powder on their faces and clipped away bits of wool here and there to make their fleeces look neater. The hinds, too, were for ever toshing up their horses, combing their manes, brushing their tails, and polishing their harness.

Jessie did not believe in gilding the lily. 'A guid scrub wi' soap an' waitter' was as far as she would go. I sometimes tried putting self-raising flour on my freckled nose, following the herd's example with the sheep, but she soon rubbed it off. 'Floor'll no' cover your sins. An' what's wrang wi' a wheen fernytickles, onyway?'

I remember once giving her a bottle of cheap scent at Christmas. She sniffed at it and made a wry face – it was certainly very strong – before putting back the cork and saying, 'Mercy me! it wad knock ye doon.'

I found the bottle days after in the duster drawer, and for ages the dusters smelt so strongly of perfume that they had to be washed in the boiler and hung on the line to get rid of Ashes of Violet. The next time I bought Jessie a present it was a bar of carbolic soap, and she was better pleased with that.

It was hardly worth my while doing good deeds or trying to improve folk, so often my plans went wrong. Yet I felt I ought to do something about the strange woman whose cottage door I used to pass every day on the way to the village school. She had a name, I suppose, but I just thought of her as Mrs Pot Plant, for she seemed to spend most of her time taking care of a sickly-looking aspidistra.

It was like a spoiled bairn; indeed, I often wondered if Mrs Pot Plant would have made such a fuss of the aspidistra if she had not been childless. She was always bringing it to the door for a breath of air, or polishing its pot. And her spirits rose and fell depending on how the plant was looking. She used to talk about it as if it was human. I would not have been surprised if she had given it a name, Wullie or Geordie.

I tried to slink past her door, for I always felt embarrassed when she brought me into the conversation. I was fond enough of plants but not to that extent.

'D'ye no' think he's lookin' doon-in-the-mooth this mornin'?' she would ask me anxiously.

'No, no; he's fine,' I would say, just to cheer her up.

But if I was not feeling fine myself, if I had the sneezes or the sniffles, Mrs Pot Plant would not let me come within coughing-distance of her precious pet.

'Watch oot,' she would warn me, 'ye micht smit him.'

Sometimes I overheard her talking encouragingly to the aspidistra. 'Come on, noo, cheer up. See! I'll set ye on the windy-sill an' ye'll get a sook o' fresh air. D'ye fancy a wee drink o' cauld tea?'

She had tried everything, she told me. Setting the plant near the fire to keep him warm, putting him through in the best room away from draughts, propping up his leaves with sticks, and giving him strange concoctions to drink in the hope that they would act as tonics. But still the aspidistra drooped and dwindled as if he was in the last stages of consumption.

Then one day a terrible tragedy happened. The pet lamb had followed me right down the road, and I was trying to shoo him away back home when he suddenly swerved and made a dive at the aspidistra which was sitting dejectedly outside the door. For once Mrs Pot Plant was not on guard to see the disaster, which was just as well, for my blood ran cold when I saw the lamb knocking over the pot, smashing it to pieces and scattering the soil in all directions.

As for the aspidistra, he lay dying on the doorstep, but I was too cowardly to wait for the requiem. I took to my heels and ran for my life; and for days afterwards I did a detour to avoid meeting the bereaved woman.

Then one day I forgot and came down the road past her cottage as usual. To my surprise Mrs Pot Plant greeted me as bright as a bee.

'See!' she said triumphantly. 'See what's happened to him.'

She pointed proudly to the aspidistra sitting in a new pot on the window-sill, looking sturdier than I had ever seen him before, with glossy leaves and his head held high.

'He's come on a treat since his accident. I thought he was a goner, but he's never looked back. D'ye no' think he's improved?'

'Oh y-yes! Yes, he has,' I agreed, and went hastily on my way, not sure whether I could take the praise or the blame. All the same, I thought it safer in future to keep detouring past her door.

5. Away to Edinburgh

It was Jessie who broke the astounding news to me. She always knew everything before I did.

'I hear ye'll be seein' Auld Reekie the morn.'

'Auld Reekie! Who's he?'

'He's no' a he. He's a place. Auld Reekie's the nickname for Edinburgh. Ye ken that, shairly. Ye're to gang there for the day. Wi' them.'

Them being my father and mother.

I would have turned a cartwheel on the spot at the thought of such an exciting adventure if I had not been feeding a calf at the time. No easy matter. The creature was half-drowning in the pail I was holding up to his head. Now and again he would extract himself and look up at me with limpid eyes before slobbering at my fingers. It was a messy performance, with the milk dribbling from the calf's mouth and running up my sleeve.

'Sook, sook', Jessie urged him. 'Mind your manners. Sook, sook.'

As soon as I could, I laid down the pail and jumped into the air like a daft thing. Fancy me going to Edinburgh, the capital of Scotland! It was the height of bliss to go to Jedburgh once in a while and see half a dozen folk in the High Street. What would it be like in Princes Street with real crowds, not to mention tramcars?

It was no wonder I could not settle to anything for the rest of that day, but wandered about like a knotless thread, visualizing the joys to come. The castle, the One o'Clock Gun, Holyrood House, Sir Walter Scott's Monument, Edinburgh Rock.

That night my mother laid out my best clothes and said, 'You'd better get to bed early. We'll have to be up at the crack.'

I hardly slept a wink, I was away in Auld Reekie all night. The crack came at the darkest hour before the dawn, and I rose bleary-eyed, feeling I was in a dream world, eating my breakfast by lamplight with my Sunday hat on my head.

The cocks were crowing and the hinds plodding up the road on their way to work when we passed them in the gig on the way down. Flora was as frisky as a flea at that hour in the morning and whisked us in to Jedburgh in record time, stopping only once at a drinking-trough by the wayside. We drove down the High Street, past the Grammar School where I was soon to be a pupil, and into the station yard where the pony was unyoked and led away to be stabled.

The train stood waiting for us, getting up steam for the journey ahead, huffing and puffing like a giant smoking a great pipe. I sat on the faded red cushions in the old three-a-side carriage and stared at the long mirror opposite. Crude coloured pictures hung above it, depicting bracing North Berwick, beautiful Inverness, and lovely Largs, all of which one could visit by train, but not on this single line.

The station-master looked in at the window to have a word with my parents and passed the usual silly remark about me, 'My! isn't she shooting up!' as if I was a beanstalk.

Then he blew his whistle, waved his flag, and we were off.

The engine let out a great mouthful of steam as we went chugging along by the riverside, with red-hot sparks flying through the air like small stars. We ran through fields, past woods and cottages. A woman hanging out her washing waved and I waved back, thinking, 'Poor soul! what a dull life she leads compared with me. Away to Edinburgh in a train!' Then, as it gathered speed, the wheels changed their tune and the scenery rushed past at such a rate it was all merged into one.

All of a sudden there was a fearsome shriek as the engine tore into a tunnel, leaving us in blank darkness. Bracing North Berwick, beautiful Inverness and lovely Largs all were blacked out. I held my breath, wondering if we would ever emerge at the other end. It seemed ages before I could see daylight ahead.

Somewhere along the line we got out, crossed over a bridge and stood on a platform awaiting the big train that would whirl us to the Waverley station. There were others sitting three-a-side when we got it, and I was separated from my parents, sitting between a man reading his paper and a woman with the hiccups.

The newspaper restricted my view, expecially when the man held it at arm's length and shook it out before rustling over another page. Every now and then the woman hiccuped when I least expected it, almost bouncing me off my seat. If Jessie had been here she would certainly have shoved a cold key down the sufferer's back and said, 'Haud your braith, wumman.'

I could have stayed happily in the Waverley station all day when we reached it, there was so much to see; but I was forced to follow my parents up the windy steps and out into the street. Princes Street. No longer just a name. A reality at last.

I had never seen a crowd before except a flock of sheep. They all had the same faces, though Jock-the-herd could tell the difference, but here there was no mistaking the individual identity of every single person hurrying along the pavements in their hundreds. How on earth – or in heaven – had God managed to make them all so different, without ever repeating the pattern? Each face was distinctive; not a shape, size or contour the same. The only thing they had in common was the careless way they strayed across the street in the teeth of the traffic. Jock would have had a hard job rounding them up with Jed and Jess.

The thing that surprised me most as we set off along Princes Street was that we met the minister. Imagine seeing a kent face in that alien throng! There he was, coming towards us, raising his hat and looking as astonished as we were. He stopped and conversed with my parents while I got bumped in different directions by the passers-by. Then we went our separate ways; but we talked about it for days afterwards.

'Fancy meeting *him*! In Edinburgh, of all places.' As if we had been to the ends of the earth.

I would have been content to stand and stare at the passing scene. Especially at a small girl jumping on to a tramcar with a schoolbag on her back. How I envied her and wished there were tramlines all the way from our farm to Jedburgh. It would be better than going to school by baneshaker.

'Come on; you'll get lost.'

My parents kept tugging me along with them. I had a feeling, as I often did, that I was being a nuisance and that they would have got on better without me. I tried hard not to lag behind, but how could I help gawping with so many unusual sights to see? A coal-black man, surely the King of the Coconut Islands, striding along the street in a white nightgown. A lordly-looking lady with a monocle, dressed in knee-britches and sporting a feather, like Coltart's, in her hat. A woman swathed in furs and carrying a trembling poodle in her arms. A Russian princess? Nothing like these could be seen around the farmyard at home. Every strange face was untapped territory, like a new book to be read.

We stopped and looked at the windows of a large shop called Jenner's. The dummy ladies gazed vacantly back at us, smiling their sweet set smiles. They wore elegant garments with price-tags on them. Pink flounced nightgowns, evening-dresses glittering with sequins, fur-lined velvet capes. Even the little girls with their golden ringlets were dressed in silks and laces, not a hair out of place, not a wrinkle in their stockings. If only I could look like that!

We went inside. The door was held open for us by a man in splendid uniform with a row of medals on his chest. Another grand gentleman dressed in tail-coats came forward and bowed to my mother as if she were a duchess. I felt she ought to have curtseyed back.

'What would you like to see, madam?'

'Gloves,' said mother firmly.

I felt proud of her as she sat at the counter on a little gilt chair, throwing back her veil and trying on one pair after another. Father wandered away to look at lum hats, and I had a feeling we would never see him again, but he came back after a while, carrying a mysterious parcel, and paid for my mother's purchases.

The prim sales-lady rolled up the money and screwed it into a wooden container, like a round cricket-ball, before sending it on its journey along an overhead railway. I watched, fascinated, till it disappeared from sight and waited till it came rolling back with the change. I wished Bella Confectionery at the village shop would deal with my halfpennies in the same way.

Afterwards we entered a lift which shot upwards, stopping at each floor to let the people in and out, with a great clanging of gates. 'Boots!' shouted the man in charge. 'Perambulators! Carpets! Curtains!' What fun to ride up and down with him all day.

I was kitted out with a sensible navy-blue coat for school – no silks and laces for me – and new shoes, to be posted on later. 'Overton Bush,' instructed my mother. 'Near Camptown, Jedburgh, Roxburghshire.' It seemed a world away and I felt almost homesick at the sound of it.

We went up the Bridges to have lunch in another big store where there was a restaurant. A three-piece orchestra, better than our gramophone at home, played sweet music above the clatter of cutlery. I admired the way the deft waitresses in their frilly white aprons and caps carried their laden trays without even dropping a saucer. The Cairthorse, I felt sure, would have smashed the whole lot in no time.

I did not eat much, I was too busy watching the people. My parents, too, gazed around and made comments.

'I wonder who she is?' mused my mother, seeing a well-dressed lady at another table. 'She looks somebody. That's a smart hat.'

'I've got a better one here,' said Father, patting the parcel at his feet.

'What? Did you buy yourself a new tile?'

'No, it's for you.'

'Oh, John!' protested my mother; but I could tell how pleased she was by the pinkness in her cheeks. The strange thing was, Father could always buy her a hat that suited her. The right shape, the right size, with a little bit of dash about it. Whenever he went to the big town without her, he never came back without one, and never once had a failure. What did he say to the sales-lady? Did he try on the hat himself? I often wondered, but he never let on.

'What colour?' asked Mother, trying not to sound too eager. 'Blue?'

'Wait and see.'

It was brown with a little frill of pheasant feathers round it, but I did not discover that till next day when I saw it on her dressing-table at home. Meanwhile there were better things to do than look at hats. When we emerged into the street the One o'Clock Gun went off with such a sudden explosion that I nearly jumped out of my skin.

Edinburgh folk had funny ways of telling the time. We went to look at the Floral Clock in Princes Street gardens, ticking slowly round under its weight of blossoms. There was little chance to examine anything closely, for we were always on the move, bound for a place called Corstorphine where the zoo was, and before that to make a duty-call on the Misses Somebody who lived near the Meadows.

The Meadows were not meadows like ours at home, with cattle and sheep grazing on them. The grass was trodden into the ground and a few people wandered around, walking their dogs. Perhaps they had a feeling they were 'in the country', even though they could hear the din of the traffic nearby.

The old ladies we were to visit lived in a crescent. It was a new name to me and I wondered if it might be some strange kind of dwelling, like an igloo, maybe, or a mud hut, but it turned out to be a flat in a curved row of houses. Very ordinary except for the magic gate.

We went there in a bus. I could have ridden in it all day round Edinburgh, catching glimpses of Sir Walter on his monument, of tramcars swaying past, and watching the conductor ringing his bell to let the people on and off. It surprised me to see a man sitting across the passage from me, reading a book. With all that stirring life going on around him! Much though I loved reading, I would not have missed a moment of it.

When we reached the locked gate in the crescent Father peered at the names, then pressed a bell to let the Misses Somebody know we had arrived. Presently the gate swung open as if an unseen hand had unlatched it, and we went in, up steep stone stairs, past other flats till we reached the right door where an elderly servant was waiting for us.

Miss Jeannie and Miss Kate were distantly related to my father, second cousins, I think. I could scarcely see them in their darkened drawing-room. Heavy lace curtains dimmed the daylight, and even the old-fashioned furniture seemed sunk in gloom. A depressed-looking canary hung in a cage near the window, hiding its head, poor thing, under its feathers.

Miss Jeannie rose to greet us, creaking as she moved, but Miss Kate sat still with her feet on a footstool and an ebony stick by her side. She had a little black beard which attracted my attention. I kept staring at it till my mother nudged me and told me to go and sit on a small chair near the canary.

We had been invited for a cup of tea and that is literally what we got. It was served with great ceremony in such delicate cups that I was petrified lest I dropped mine and was disgraced for ever. The servant brought in the tray, spread a fine lace cloth on a small table, and Miss Jeannie took charge of the silver teapot. There were little tongs for the sugar-lumps and a strainer through which she poured the tea, puckering up her lips and taking care not to spill a single drop.

Grown-up conversation went on, mainly about the health of the old ladies, but I did not listen. I was trying to read the titles of the books locked in the glass-fronted bookcase. They looked as if they had never been read. Sets of the Waverley novels in dark red bindings, the *History of the World*, encyclopedias, sermons and dull-looking volumes of Shakespeare's works.

Suddenly my eyes lit on a shabbier book with a more familiar title, *Little Women*. I longed to unlock the bookcase and let it out, and looked across at the old ladies, wondering if they had ever shed tears over Beth, or laughed at Jo's exploits. But it seemed unlikely that they could ever have given way to such foolishness.

When it was time to go, Miss Kate beckoned me to her beaded footstool, fumbled in a pouch hidden amongst the folds of her skirt, and brought out a silver shilling.

'There! Take care how you spend it.'

'Oh yes, I will! Thanks!'

Miss Jeannie patted me on the head and said I was very

like somebody, but she could not remember who. I hoped it
was someone nice.

Then the servant showed us out, and we went down the
stone stairs, back through the magic gate. The visit was
over, and I took a great gulp of Edinburgh air, thankful to
be free.

I did not like the zoo. Father and mother seemed to expect
me to enjoy seeing so many strange beasts and birds, but all
I wanted was to open their cages and set them free. I would
sooner have had one of our own Clydesdales than the great
lumbering elephant with its swaying trunk. I refused to
ride on its back, and took a scunner at the gorillas grinning
at me through their bars. I wanted to get back to the shops
to spend the silver shilling.

We went back in a tramcar and had a proper tea in a
Princes Street tea-room, looking out towards the castle.
The waitress brought a three-tiered dish with scones on the
top, pancakes and currant bread in the middle, and little
iced cakes on the bottom. One worked one's way down
from plain to fancy. It was like a dream, looking up at the
battlements and eating pink icing at the same time.

After such an early morning start I was beginning to feel
drowsy, and for the rest of the day I went about in a daze,
not sure that I was really awake. Everything seemed to have
grown bigger, noisier and more confusing: the clang of the
tramcars, the roar of the traffic, the tramping of feet. I
seemed far away from reality and began to long for a sight
of the quiet hills at the Back of Beyond.

On the way back to the Waverley station we went into
a shop to buy some Edinburgh Rock. Which colour to
choose? White, gingery brown, pale pink? Around the
shelves there were hundreds of bottles of strange sweet-
meats never seen in Bella's shop. It would have been great
to stay there and sample the lot.

In the train I held the little box of rock in its tartan wrap-
pings on my knee, and tried to resist the temptation to

open it. I wanted to save some for Jessie, the herd, and Liz-Ann. Now and again my fingers fumbled with the paper, then the train gave a jerk and slid out of the station. Before long the rhythm of the wheels acted as a soporific, and I fell asleep sitting bolt upright.

I awoke in a fright to find myself in pitch darkness. Had I died and gone to the Bad Place? There was a flash of fire, a flurry of sparks, and suddenly the train rushed out of a tunnel. For the rest of the journey I stayed wide awake, watching the lit windows and wondering what the folk were doing inside their houses. Eating their suppers, maybe, or reading the paper before going to bed.

At long last I was back in my accustomed seat in the gig, with Flora kicking up her heels as she cantered home. It seemed years since we had made the reverse journey in the early morning, and I felt I had lived through a lifetime of experiences since then.

It was so late that we met no one on the way. There was nothing to be seen except the sheep's eyes shining from the fields. The night air was keen, as sharp as soor dook. It kept me from nodding off and falling out.

Then suddenly the pony turned in at our road-end and my heart gave a little leap. We were back on our own home ground. It had been exciting seeing all the glories of the great city, but it was nice to know the shabby old farmhouse awaited us. Maybe I would get tired of Princes Street, never of our own homestead.

6. Into the Unknown

I thought I knew everything till I went to the Grammar School and learnt that I knew nothing.

Had I not passed my Qualifying? I could milk a cow, stook corn, feed calves, turn the heel of a sock, read anything from the *Scotsman* to the *Pilgrim's Progress*. I knew a stirk from a stot, a yowe from a gimmer, and had even been to Edinburgh for the day.

But I had never heard of algebra or science. Or of those strange marks called circumflexes over unpronounceable French words. Indeed, the first word I learned was a Latin one. Ignoramus. It described me, according to my new teachers, and was only a different way of telling me I had no rummlegumption.

It was frightening on that first morning going down the rough farm road knowing I was not on my way to join my former classmates. For the first time in my life I felt homesick, not so much for home as for a sight of my familiar desk at the old school. Even old Baldy-Heid in a rage would have been a pleasanter prospect than the un-known terrors awaiting me in the town.

The cottage wives turned the screw as I walked past, self-conscious in my new togs: navy-blue gym-tunic, white blouse, navy-blue coat, new shoes that hurt after running barefoot all summer. I was even wearing a pair of gloves.

'Look at her!' said Mrs Thingummy – I could never remember the names of the hinds' wives – shaking her rag rug and barely visible behind a cloud of dust. Where did it come from every day? 'A' dressed up! She'll soon get the stuffin' taken oot her.'

'So she wull,' agreed the other Mrs Thingummy, dole-fully. I never saw *her* shaking a rug. She was more often hanging out her man's long drawers and flannel shirts on the line. 'She little kens what she's in for, puir cratur'.'

Thus encouraged, I went off to my execution with lagging steps, but brightened up when I saw Jock-the-herd leaning over a dyke.

'Man-lassie,' he shouted, taking no notice of my new outfit, 'see that black-faced yowe? Could ye weir her in through the yett?'

'Yes, I could, Jock.'

For a few blissful moments, during which I lost a hair-ribbon and one of my gloves, I forgot my impending doom. If only I could have changed places with the collies and spent the rest of the day rounding up sheep! But the school bus was to come for me at the road-end, and I had been warned not to be late, especially on my first day.

No need, after all, to travel by pony or by bicycle. It was a relief to me when I heard about the bus which was to collect me and several other scholars at road-ends on the way in to Jedburgh. I waited for it outside Mary-Anne's lodge-house at the corner while she fed her hens and talked to them, as Mrs Pot Plant did to her aspidistra. Maggie, Mrs Broon, Jemima, Wee Rascal, and the rest. She had a name for the cockerel, too. His Nibs.

Mary-Anne was like a wee wizened apple, all wrinkled and with only one tooth. The pockets of her apron were always full of corn or new-laid eggs.

'Maggie's aff her meat,' she told me, looking disconsolately at one of her drooping hens. 'She's feelin' a bit upsy-doonsy. Nae appetite. What aboot a jeelly-piece?'

If Maggie had no appetite, mine was sharp enough in the early morning to do justice to the slice of pan-loaf spread with rasp jam when Mary-Anne brought it out to me. I never ate much at meal-times but was always ready for 'shivery-bites' in between.

As I was licking the jam off my fingers, Big Bob, the braggart at the village school, came along, kicking a stone in front of him. I would have given anything to fall into step beside him, even though he stuck out his tongue at me and jeered, 'Silly thing! Dressed up like mince an' tatties.'

It was a lonely feeling standing there by the roadside wondering if I would ever be picked up. But presently a small bus came rattling to a standstill beside me, and a stout red-faced driver leaned out. 'Hop in, wee ane,' said he, hauling me up the steep step as if I was a sack of potatoes, and slamming the door behind me.

I was off into the unknown.

But the great thing was, I had found a new friend. Black Sandy. I never found out how the driver came by his name. Certainly not by the colour of his hair, what was left of it, for it was as carrotty as mine. Perhaps he had been christened Sandy Black and someone had reversed it. Black Sandy he remained to me, and to the others whom he picked up on the winding road into Jedburgh.

All the way in he whistled like a linty and sang at the pitch of his voice. 'The Muckin' o', Geordie's Byre', 'The Bonnie Lass o' Fyvie', 'Paddy McGinty's Goat'. When he ran short of songs, he had a shot at hymns. 'By Cool Siloam's Shady Rill', 'Onward Christian Soldiers', 'Abide With Me'.

He would shout, too, at the bus as if it was a horse. 'Whoa there! Steedy! Gee-up, auld cuddy!' He was great.

The best thing about Black Sandy was his sense of justice. He did not mind how much din we made in the bus, and we made plenty for we were a boisterous lot, but if I was getting the worst of it, he would roar over his shoulder, 'Leave the wee ane alane, or I'll clout ye on the lug.'

It worked both ways. I always stood up for the portly driver when the others became cheeky and shouted abuse at him.

> Black Sandy,
> His legs are bandy.

'No, they're not,' I would protest, and put up my fists, ready for battle.

Black Sandy himself did not seem to mind the insults.

> Sticks an' stanes'll break ma banes
> But words'll never hurt me.

He could have hurt any of us with one sweep from his powerful arms, but it never came to that. His threats were enough.

On that first day I rattled about in the empty bus like a loose pea in a pod before Black Sandy drew up at the roadside to collect his next passenger. His stops and starts were so jerky that I was often black and blue by the end of the journey; but he always got us there even in the iciest days of winter when he had to put chains on the wheels and we were often ordered to get out and push.

There were about a dozen of us in the bus by the time we passed the old Capon Tree, the last giant of Jedforest, and came within sight of the ruined abbey. After rattling down the High Street, Black Sandy drew up at the school gates. 'Whoa, auld cuddy! Oot, everybody!' he shouted. I had reached the point of no return.

I began my Higher Education with a blot. Worse, I

dropped a ruler with such a clatter it attracted the attention of my first new teacher and foiled my main object, which was to keep quiet and not be noticed.

'Fumble-fingers!' she said, pointing me out to the rest of the class. 'You, the gingery one.'

I had often been called Carrot-heid at the village school. Now I was Ginger. Not that names mattered. It took me weeks to get the hang of what the teachers were called. There were so many of them, and we were constantly coming and going from one classroom to another. No sooner, it seemed, had we got settled to one lesson, than a bell would ring. All change! We had to pick up books and pencils, troop off to another room and turn our minds to an entirely different subject, taught by yet another strange teacher. I was bamboozled for weeks before I settled into the routine.

The first teacher was an indomitable character called Miss Crichton, who came from the North-East and taught us French in an Aberdeen accent. Later on, when a real Frenchman came to visit the school, I thought he could not speak the language for toffee. His accent was so different from ours.

On that first morning I never got further than *la* and *le*. It seemed daft to me that a table should be feminine and a ceiling masculine, but if Miss Crichton said so it must be true, for she spoke with such authority and emphasized every word by blowing her nose. She was troubled, poor soul, with persistent catarrh and was for ever drying her handkies on the radiator. But for all that she was a born teacher and dinned the learning into us with many a rap over the head with a long pointer.

All that day I went in a daze from history to English, algebra to science, with my mind becoming more and more muddled. I longed to be back in Auld Baldy-Heid's domain, where I could sit in peace doodling on my jotter while he taught the little ones their poetry.

> I have a little shadow that goes in and out with me,
> And what can be the use of it is more than I can see.

It seemed a lifetime before we were let out into the vast playground for a break. There were no communal games of kick-the-can or hide-and-seek. The laddies went their own ways, playing with a real football, while the lasses leant limply against a wall, or played a half-hearted game of rounders.

They looked upon me, rightly enough, as 'in from the country'. No doubt they thought I lived in a byre or a hen-house. Indeed, I felt like a shaggy sheep-dog beside them, and kept my distance, humbly grateful if they allowed me to retrieve a ball that had fallen at my feet.

Then one of them called: 'Hi, Ginger! Catch!' I was in!

Many of the pupils went home for their midday meals, but those from a distance ate their pieces in the playground, and could buy a steaming-hot bowl of soup for a penny from a vast cauldron in one of the sheds. It was boiled up and ladled out by a wee woman who called us all You.

'Come on, You! Haud oot your bowel!'

The soup was thick and tasty, full of fresh vegetables. A meal in itself. But if we preferred 'rubbish', as I often did, we could go out into the street and look for the nearest sweet-shop. Or buy an ice-cream slider at the Tally's shop up near the market-place.

It was a long time before I was bold enough to leave the safe precincts of the playground and venture out into the town on my own. A fearsome man called the Janny guarded the gates and ruthlessly locked them the moment the school bell summoned us back for the afternoon session.

What if one got left outside? No use looking imploringly through the bars, or trying to climb over. The gates were too high, and the janitor deaf to all pleas. Timing, therefore, was of first importance, and I had no watch. The town clock was up in the market-place, but could one be certain that it was always at the right time?

After a while I overcame my anxieties and took my first tentative steps to freedom. Thereafter a whole new world was opened to me as I explored the streets, closes, and back alleyways. I could never get over the excitement of being let loose in a town, of watching people, seeing the shops, hearing other sounds than the crowing of cocks and bleating of sheep, of finding treasure-trove every time I turned a corner.

The house, for example, where Bonnie Prince Charlie sought refuge during the Forty-Five. I stood gawping at it, picturing him riding into the town at the head of his band of wild Highlanders, looking for recruits. If I had been there at the time I would have joined him in a jiffy.

The town was full of history, better than the dull contents of the lesson-books in the Grammar School. Sometimes I stood on the ramparts and gazed sadly at the ruined abbey, thinking of the skirmishes which took place when the old enemy came over the Border to ransack the place. Or I looked up at a little window in Queen Mary's House, half-expecting to see a sad sweet face looking out and a lily-white hand waving to me.

Down at the Townfoot Brig I could lean over and look at the ducking-place where suspected witches were tested in the old days. If they sank they were innocent. If they floated they were guilty and burned alive. There was no hope for them either way, poor things.

One day in my wanderings round the town I found the house at Abbey Close where Wordsworth of the dancing daffodils, and his sister Dorothy, had lodged.

As I was staring at it a little man in a long ragged coat came and stood beside me. A wandering tramp, maybe, for his pouches seemed to contain all his worldly possessions. He talked half to himself, half to me, in an English accent.

One of the auld enemy clan. But I could forgive him that, since he was so full of information.

'Did you know that Sir Walter Scott visited the Wordsworths when they stayed here? No? Well, he did. And, what's more, he read his new poem to them. *The Lay of the Last Minstrel*. In this very house.

> 'The way was long, the wind was cold,
> The minstrel was infirm and old. . . .'

He went on, stanza after stanza. Then he took off his bonnet. At first I thought it was a gallant gesture in honour of Sir Walter, but when he held it out to me I saw that he wanted recompense and had to fumble in my pocket for my penny. There was no ice-cream or sweets for me that day, but it was well worth the sacrifice. I felt that I was personally acquainted with Sir Walter and the Wordsworths for ever after.

Later on I learned that Robert Burns had also come to Jedburgh with his head full of poetry, and true to form had wandered by the banks of the Jed with a bonnie lassie. I considered it remiss of Shakespeare not to have visited the town, and thought he might have written even better plays if he had come.

As always, though, it was people rather than places that mattered most. I loved the Cross, the hub of the universe, where multitudes it seemed to me foregathered on market-day. I might see my father there surrounded by his cronies, all laughing uproariously at some of his quips. Father's funny stories were the talk of the countryside. It was not so much the stories themselves as the way he told them. I knew them all word for word but I could have listened to him for ever.

I did not go near him, of course. The market-place was not for females; but if he caught sight of me standing on the pavement he would come across, thrust his hand into his pocket and bring forth some coppers to spend.

'There, lass!'

That was all he said before rejoining his fellow farmers at the Cross. But it left a warm glow at my heart, and it was not only because of the pennies.

It was a bonus if I met my mother in the High Street, dressed in her fur coat and wearing the hat Father had bought her in Edinburgh. I felt proud to be walking by her side, especially if one of the town scholars saw us together. Maybe I was only a tousled tyke from the country, but my mother looked a lady. I felt my stock rising if she walked me down as far as the school gates. Even the Janny touched his cap to her.

But these were rare occasions. Mostly I was on my own, content to roam from the Castlegate to the Bow, from Duck Row to the Friars (I got to know all the names eventually) but always rushing back to the market-place so that I could keep an eye on the town clock.

All this was far in the future. On that first day I was too bemused to stray out of step. I kept in line with the others, following them like a sheep from one classroom to another. By the time the final bell rang I could not believe it was only that same morning I had walked down the farm road and helped Jock with his stray yowe.

Black Sandy was waiting with his bus at the school gate. 'Hop in, wee ane,' he said, giving me a mighty heave up. 'Onward Christian Soldiers!'

We were off on the road home.

I got out at the Camptown road end and walked the mile back to the farm, trying to untangle all the new experiences that were whirling through my head. What a lot I would have to tell everybody! All about *la table*, the janitor, and the science master who called me miss. 'Come on, miss. Look lively. Have you never seen a Bunsen burner before?' Indeed, I had not.

I came down to earth with a bump. It was a great blow to find the whole household was not waiting breathlessly for my return. They were all too engrossed in their own pursuits to show any interest in mine. Jessie was out milking the cows, the servant-lassie was scouring the churn and did not even look at me when I came in. My mother was ben the hoose whirring away at the sewing-machine.

'There's some supper in the oven,' she called through, and that was all.

So in the end I sat down at *la* kitchen *table* to my solitary meal, dumped in spirits but realizing that amongst all the lessons I had learned that day, the hardest was that I must continue to plough a lonely furrow.

What a lot one had to keep to oneself for the lack of a listening ear. But there was always an inner self with whom one could share experiences. So as I ate my mince and cabbage I went over it all again in my own head.

When Jessie came clattering in with the milk-pails, she asked, 'Hoo did ye get on, lassie?' But by now I wanted to keep it to myself, so I just said, 'Fine.'

7. Men and Beasts

I was now a town mouse as well as a country one, living in two dimensions, travelling to Jedburgh every day and coming back up the bumpy road to the farm every evening.

The things I knew! *Ouvrez la porte.* Isosceles triangles. The exports of Australia. The wives of Henry the Eighth.

But I was still nobody at home, glad enough to shed my town skin with my school clothes and run wild at the weekends and during the long summer evenings. This was my real world. The other was only a confused muddle of French verbs, English essays, and dead kings.

There was a creaking swing in the wood where I sometimes sat swaying to and fro. In fits of derring-do I would try to raise enough impetus to fly as high as the treetops, frightening the cushy-doos from their perches and causing the herd to shout up to me, 'Watch oot, wumman! Ye'll drap deid!' But I could usually persuade him to give me a push, and once I even inveigled him to sit on the swing himself.

'Here! no' so high!' he roared when I shoved him off with all my might. He was so much heavier than I was that he sailed away sky-high. It was strange having Jock at my mercy. I laughed while I swung him round and round till the rope was in a twist and he whirled about as helpless as a baby, while Jed and Jess sat on their tails, their tongues hanging out in amazement.

When he was back on his feet again Jock shook his fist at me, picked up his crook and said, 'Ye wee deevil, ye! I've a guid mind to cut doon that swing.' But, of course, he never did.

I still followed at his heels like an extra collie, clambering over dykes and sometimes helping to 'shed' the sheep when he was trying to count them. This meant shooing them through a narrow opening while the herd began in a sing-song voice, 'Ane-twae-three-fower.' Often he got mixed up when the sheep darted through two at a time or doubled back on their tracks. Then he would give a groan and say, 'Was that toonty-fower or toonty-five? Dammit! I'm a' mixed up.'

I liked to hear the Northumbrian shepherds counting their flock. None of your one-two-three-four. They had a kind of rigmarole which I learnt off by heart.

> Een-teen-tethera-methera-pimp.
> Awfus-dawfus-deefus-dumfus-dik.
> Een-a-dik, teen-a-dik. . . .

On to bumpit and jiggit. A much better way of doing arithmetic than bothering about vulgar fractions.

Jock had various evil-smelling medicines with which he doctored sick animals from time to time, but there were occasions when a horse or a cow developed some serious ailment which necessitated a visit from the vet.

He was a big bluff man who came all the way from Kelso, driving a rattletrap of a motor car as if it was a charger. He had the reputation of being fond of a dram, and after ministering to the sick beast he always came into the house with my father for a secret refreshment.

I kept out of his way, for he was a jokey man, given to great gusts of laughter at my expense, and I was never sure whether his leg-pulls were real or not. If I was within reach, he would grab me by the hair, brandish a fearsome-looking instrument from his bag and roar, 'Is this the patient? Right! I'll soon cure her. Off with her top knot!' He was terrifying.

But Jock said he had a wonderful way with beasts and could make them understand what he was saying. I wondered what kind of noises he made when communicating with a cow or a Clydesdale, but I was much too frightened of him to find out. It was said, true or not, that he used to drive through gates without bothering to open them, charging at them in his rattletrap and not caring what wreckage he left behind.

We were used to having ailing animals in the kitchen. Lambs needing to be bottle-fed, a sick calf that lay on the rug beside the cat, or drooping chicks which we wrapped in flannel and popped like pies into the gently heated oven. As soon as they revived and we heard their cheep-cheeps, we took them out and let them stagger about on the floor. Before long they were pecking at crumbs or snuggling down beside Blackie, the kitchen cat, who accepted any strange bedfellows that came her way.

Blackie was different from the other cats who roamed around the farmyard, superior to them in that she had the run of the house, and above average, too, in intelligence. Her greatest feat was to open the kitchen door.

The first time it happened we were all startled out of our skins. Suddenly the door swung open, like the magic gate in Edinburgh, and in walked the cat as calm as could be. I ran out to see if anybody had helped her, but there was no one there. The door had a high sneck which had to be pressed firmly to release the catch. It took me all my time to reach up to it. So how on earth had Blackie done it?

Time and again the same thing happened. In the end I waited outside to see if I could solve the mystery. There was a high garden wall by the kitchen door, adjacent to it. Blackie sat there, sunning herself as a change from basking at the kitchen fire. Then suddenly she rose and stretched herself. She had had enough fresh air for the day. Time to go inside.

The door was firmly shut, but Blackie knew what to do. She gathered herself together, took a sideways spring, twisted herself round in mid air, and pressed her paws down on the sneck. Clever thing! But she did not succeed at the first attempt. It was a case of try-try-try again. Down she fell on to the doorstep, and back she leapt on to the wall, to go through the whole performance over and over again, maybe a dozen times, without ever wearying. Persistence paid, for the door finally swung open. Blackie arched her tail proudly and stalked in. I felt she ought to be in the history-books, like Bruce and the spider.

The outside cats were a mixed lot, supposed to wage war on the rats and mice that infested the farmyard, but always turning up in the byre at milking time. My own favourite was the small white kitten who sat next to me and mieowed up at me as if telling me all her troubles. I mieowed back at her and we got on a treat.

Every now and then one of the cats would seek a safe hiding-place where she could produce yet another brood of fluffy kittens.

'We'll need to droon them,' said Jessie, but with no great conviction She even allowed Blackie to 'kittle' in the cupboard below the stairs, and for ages afterwards we were stepping over small squeaking creatures crawling about on the kitchen floor

One of my favourite friends was a small brown bantam hen, the wee banty. She laid the smallest egg, which was lost in an ordinary egg-cup; but I had a special one, not much bigger than a thimble, just the right size to hold the brown banty's offering.

Everything about her was tiny, except her courage. She would even turn on the bubblyjock and chase after him if he was pestering me. The same with her husband, the bantam cockerel. She would rush at him with her small wings outstretched and every feather bristling with rage, chasing him round the farmyard till he cried for mercy.

It was not every day the wee banty laid an egg for my tea, but when she did, it was like playing hide-and-seek, trying to find it. She never went near the henhouse, but had secret laying-places of her own in the corner of the byre or by the side of a hayrick, sometimes even in the pigsty.

But often the banty could not keep the secret to herself. After laying an egg she would come peck-pecking at the kitchen door.

'Wha's that?' Jessie would say, listening with her head to one side. 'It canna be the postie; it's no' lood enough. It'll be that banty o' yours. Ye'd better gang an' find oot if she's laid.'

So out I would go, and the banty would strut away in front of me, clucking to herself and looking back now and again to see if I was following. She never took me to the right place, but near enough. It was all part of the game. Then when I finally found the small egg she would flap her wings as if clapping them. I could almost hear her clucking 'Well done!'

One day she went broody and vanished into the wood, where she had a hidden hoard of eggs on which she sat patiently till they hatched out. It was great to see her marching proudly back to the farmyard at the head of a procession of five tiny chicks.

'Cluck-cluck! Oh the cleverness of me!'

On the farm it was always a case of multiplying and subtracting. Life and death. Cows calved, horses foaled, new litters of piglets appeared, lambs were born. But their lives were short. Cattle and sheep were taken away to be sold, Grumphy met his sad fate, and cocks and hens had their necks drawn.

I wondered if they all went to heaven.

'Och aye! nae doot there's a special place for beasts,' Jessie assured me.

'Who looks after them?' I wanted to know.

'Moses, maybe. Or ane o' thon disciples.'

'Which one?'

'Hoots! they tak' turns. Get oot ma road.'

All the beasts on the farm seemed to have bottomless stomachs and no set meal-times. They pecked and chewed all day long. There was little else for them to do, poor things, not even a book to read. I felt especially sorry for the cows who lay amongst the buttercups and daisies for long monotonous hours, with no other diversion than swallowing their cud.

I wondered if I ought to organize some activity to take them out of themselves, games perhaps. Surely they could run races or play with a tennis-ball, tossing it to each other with their horns. But if I approached them, all they did was get up and wander away to lie down on a fresh patch of grass and continue their chewing. It seemed to fulfil all their needs, so what was the use of trying to improve their lot? At least they did not have to trouble their heads about isosceles triangles.

I never had any desire to tame a wild creature or trap a bird in a cage, nor could I understand the town-folk who kept dogs as pets, making them sit up and beg for a biscuit and taking them out on a lead. 'Good doggy! Come for walkies!' Farm animals, at least, were free.

The day I hated most was when Father held a 'shoot'. His sporting friends, dressed in knickerbockers and stout boots, would come with their guns, game-bags, and retrievers to stride over the heathery hill, with the hinds and the herd acting as beaters. All day long I heard the death-knell in the distance, the cracking of shots, the screaming of pheasants, the baying of dogs.

Meantime the house was astir with activity. Feverish preparations were being made for a great feast to greet the return of the hungry hunters. The largest ashets, platters, and soup tureens were brought out, the dining-room table spread with a white cloth, and the best cutlery laid at each place. Great roasts of mutton were sizzling in the oven, mountains of potatoes had been peeled, and a big pot of turnips was on the boil. A cauldron of soup hung on the swey over the kitchen fire.

There had been a great baking of apple pies, gooseberry tarts and puddings. And one of Mother's special trifles, laced with sherry and topped with whipped cream, was cooling in the milkhouse.

The sideboard was already laden with dishes, carving-knives, jugs of cream, sauce-boats, the cheese dish, the bread board, and sundry extras such as plates of scones and short-bread to fill up odd corners. Though how anyone could have a corner to spare after such a feed was beyond my comprehension. But killing seemed to sharpen the appetite, and the hunters were ravenous enough to eat several helpings of everything when they returned from the slaughter.

My task was to fill the cruets. A fikey job, Jessie said, and so it was. I had to clean and polish the big silvery one, wash the china set in soapy water and clear out any salt that had caked in the bottom. No matter how careful I was with the pepper I always ended up sneezing; and if I spilt any salt I always flung a pinch over my left shoulder to keep bad luck at bay.

Sometimes, too, I was set to work with a pair of wooden 'bats' to roll the butter into little round pats. And what a performance that was, dipping the bats into hot water to prevent the butter from sticking. I could never see the point of it. Butter was butter, and would the men care what shape it was?

At the darkening, when the last shot had been heard, the flurried activity in the kitchen reached a crescendo, with an opening of oven doors, a stirring of pans, a champing of potatoes. Faces became redder, and Mother hastily changed into her best blouse – lilac with lace down the front – while Jessie tied on a clean apron. The lamps were lit, the fires piled high with logs, and the shabby old house looked cosy and welcoming. But the men did not come straight in. We heard them in the out-house, laughing and talking, as they gutted the hares and rabbits, hung up the game birds and divided out the spoil.

At last they came trooping in, reeking of blood and gun-shot, and after a great cleaning up they settled round the dining-room table, my father at the head.

First things first. He always said grace. 'Bless this food and forgive us our sins. Amen.' If the minister was present he took over and addressed the Almighty at greater length.

I liked the Sheep's-Heid Grace, which I had heard from Jock-the-herd, though it was Robert Burns and not Jock who had composed it. What a busy man he must have been! He and Anon and Shakespeare seemed to have written almost everything between them.

> O Lord, when hunger pinches sore
> Do thou stand us in stead,
> And send us, from they bounteous store
> A tup or wether head.

While father sharpened the carving-knife the soup was dished up from the big tureen, and they were off. I acted as an extra serving-maid, fetching and carrying, getting my plaits pulled and having to put up with much boisterous banter. It seemed that in my youth nobody ever addressed a sensible word to me. I was only good for a joke. 'My, you'd make a tasty bite, lassie. Ask your Father to carve me a slice.'

I hated them all.

Yet, looking back I can see they were a nice jovial lot, appreciative of all the good food and full of compliments to my mother whose face grew more and more rosy as the evening wore on. In the back-kitchen the servant-girl was up to her elbows in soap suds, coping with the piles of dirty dishes, while Jessie, her lips set in a grim line, kept serving up more and more potatoes or extracting pies from the oven.

'If ye drap that tray I'll murder ye!'

When it was all over, the men sat back and lit up their pipes or cigars. Then the stories began. My father was the best, as always. I hardly listened to the others, but sat invisible, I hoped, on a footstool in the corner, watching.

Sometimes a rollicking sing-song started up. 'The Lum Hat Wantin' a Croon', 'Paddy McGinty's Goat', 'By Yon Bonnie Banks', with my mother joining in.

If they caught sight of me and tried to get me to do my piece, I fled to the kitchen and sat beside Blackie on the rug, listening to the bursts of laughter till Jessie chased me off to bed with my candle. When I closed my eyes all I could see were rows and rows of carcases hanging in the shed outside.

8. Out in the Wilds

'What's it like, then, away out in the wilds?'

I was constantly being asked this question by town-folk who had a strange idea of what country life was like. They were terrified, I discovered, of cows and thought pigs were filthy brutes. Some of my fellow-scholars had never even seen a hen in their lives.

Butter, eggs, and milk were commodities to be bought in a shop, all ready-made. How they got there was a mystery the town children never bothered to solve. They knew nothing about milking, mucking out a byre, churning butter, or hunting for new-laid eggs. Nor had they any idea what a tattie-bogle was, let alone a bubblyjock.

I was little more than a savage, living amongst the hills with not a neighbour within sight.

'What on earth do you do with yourself out there?'

It was difficult to explain. How could I convey the pleasures of swinging on a gate, watching a bird build its nest, feeding a calf, climbing the old oak tree, running barefoot in the flowery meadow, listening to the skylark singing? I could never find the right words to say. In any case, they already mocked my way of speaking, especially when I came away with some of Jessie's expressions. Words like donnert, dumfoonert, and peelly-wally they had never heard of; and shrieked with mirth when I referred to the tap of drinking-water in the playground as the sprigget.

'Listen to her! She's like a foreigner.'

I had to be careful, too, when speaking to the teachers, some of whom had sarcastic tongues, far more hurtful than the tawse.

'Explain yourself properly. You're in civilization now, not in the wilds.'

The wilds, always the wilds, and always a snigger from the rest of the class. No wonder I never put up my hand or volunteered an answer. It was best to remain invisible and dumb.

My worst moment came when the English teacher, a pale woman who wore high-necked blouses and long black skirts, made me come out in front of the class, as Auld Baldy-Heid had sometimes done, to read out my essay.

It was a compliment, I suppose, but I would sooner have been flung into the fiery furnace. I remember praying feverishly to God to strike me dead on the spot, but He took no notice.

I think I have seldom suffered more through all the trials and tribulations of life than on that day, forced to shuffle out and face my giggling classmates, conscious of all my deficiencies, in particular my country accent.

The essay was a fanciful affair entitled 'My Dream Holiday'. It had looked all right when I was writing it, apart from the odd blot, but now as I read it out it sounded rubbish. Who wanted to hear about my visit to an unknown country in the clouds – Skyland, I think it was called – and of my unlikely adventures running up rainbows and swinging on stars? I was shaking at the knees and red with shame as I finished. Luckily a bell rang – all change – and before anyone could make a comment the class had trooped off to algebra.

I was so used to being in the wrong that it never occurred to me to criticize the way the town-folk behaved. Yet I was beginning to find that living in a crowded community had its drawbacks. I had always longed to see different faces. Now I was seeing too many, so that I could not sort them out and place them in their proper categories.

In the country everyone was an individual. Mary-Anne and her hens, Auld Baldy-Heid, the minister, Bella at the shop, the folk on the farm, my granny in her cottage at Camptown. I had had a long time to study them and knew every wrinkle on their faces, every gesture they made, every peculiarity in their speech.

Now I was flung into a maelstrom of strangers. It was difficult enough to distinguish the teachers let alone the hundreds of pupils. But the one who stood out above them all was the headmaster.

He was known in the Grammar School as the rector, an irascible little man, very red in the face, like a volcano about to explode. His name was Mr Archibald, and he was known to all as Archie-Bald. Or Dafty, behind his back.

Dafty was as soft-footed as a cat and would suddenly appear in a classroom, watching and listening but seldom saying a word. This was the most terrifying thing about him. We never knew what he was thinking or when the explosion would take place. When it did, even the teachers looked faint. I preferred Auld Baldy-Heid who never reined in his rages.

The only lesson the rector took himself was Latin. It was an extra subject, and for some strange reason it had been decreed that I should take it. I was the only girl in my year who did; so on certain days I, along with five or six boys who were also forced to undergo the same form of purgatory, was sent off to Dafty's room to suffer the tortures of the damned.

Mr Archibald would be sitting at his desk, lost in thought. Away in a dwam, Jessie would have said. He took no notice of us, but fiddled about with a paper-clip, tapped his teeth with a ruler, and stared into space. Suddenly, and we never knew when to expect it, his eyes would focus on us, and the shouting-match would begin. Dafty never spoke. He roared. For such a small man he had the bellow of a bull.

'Man, you're an ass! Sit down, you donkey.'

I remember this above all his other expletives, directed at the boys and me alike. He never took the trouble to explain anything, just expected us to get to our feet in turn, read from our Latin primers, and that was that. It was like floundering through treacle. I never came anywhere near getting the hang of it and was frightened out of my wits most of the time. The dead language remained dead, as far as I was concerned.

There were long gaps during which Dafty retired into his shell and we were left to study our books on our own. Mine was tattered and torn, being a hand-me-down from my elder brother and sister who had evidently suffered the same tribulation in the past, according to the despairing scribbles on the fly-leaf.

'If all the world should be submerged, this book would still be dry.'

'Hear, hear,' I wrote after it.

The boys and I sometimes played noughts and crosses on the endpapers instead of learning *amo amas amat*. Later on in the book there was a piece about Balbus building a wall. As far as I know, he may still be building it.

'Man, you're an ass!' Archie-Bald would suddenly spring to life when we least expected it, and catch us flicking blotting-paper pellets at each other to break the monotony.

The lessons were sometimes enlivened by the janitor coming in with a complaint.

'Maister Archie-Bald, thae heathens have went an' broken another windy. It'll need to be seen to.'

It was better than Balbus and his wall.

We welcomed all interruptions, even when Miss Crichton or one of the other teachers dragged a reluctant pupil into the room for punishment, though we felt sorry enough for the sinner. The teachers had no straps of their own. The rector kept his own hangman's whip locked in his desk and acted as general executioner, a job he seemed to relish. It was much larger and nippier than Auld Baldy-Heid's tawse. Even the biggest boys would bite their lips and fight back their tears when the rector went into action.

Somehow we, the watchers, felt as shamed and guilty as the victim when a teacher brought him in and complained of his misdeeds.

'Cheeky, eh? Making trouble, eh?' roared Archie-Bald, his fiery face growing redder as he brought out the strap. 'I'll make trouble for *you*, boy! Hold out your hand.'

I was thankful not to be at the receiving end. Indeed, only once did I incur the full force of the rector's wrath when, in a fit of exasperation at my ignorance he hit me over the head with my primer. My hair was thick enough to withstand the blow, but half the pages fell out of the book. No great loss.

Still, in spite of his hot temper, Mr Archibald could be as gentle as a lamb when any sick pupil was brought to him. He kept smelling-salts and sticking-plaster in a drawer in his desk, and would apply bandages to bruised knees as soothingly as any nurse.

'There, there! You'll soon feel better.'

He was a study, this strange little man, as difficult to fathom as the Latin language itself. It would have been hard enough for any psychoanalyst to comprehend him, let alone me, though I used to sit looking at him and wondering what was going on in his head during his long withdrawn silences. Perhaps, like me, he had another self with whom he could communicate. Something seemed to give him a secret sense of satisfaction, for now and then a smile flickered across his face, but he soon wiped it off if he saw we were watching.

I liked the English lessons best of all, so long as Miss Pale-face ignored me and did not force me to read out my essays. She had a real love of poetry and used to recite it to us in a genteel voice.

> 'Over the cobbles he clattered and clanged
> In the pale moonlight.'

She introduced us to Oliver Twist. I lived every moment of his vicissitudes and was always away ahead of the chapter we were meant to be studying. I related it all to Jessie when I got home, and must have fired her with indignation, for I remember her clenching her fists and crying, 'If I could get ma hands on that Maister Bumble, I'd gie him what for.'

The people were as real to her as they were to me. How I envied Dickens's power to create such lifelike characters. Had *he* ever sat in a classroom, blotting his copybook? I could not imagine him writing such trivialities as 'My Dream Holiday'.

Maybe I, too, ought to try to write about real people. Not Archie-Bald, who was too complex a character, but perhaps I could write about Jessie or Jock-the-herd whom I understood better. But I could not see them as heroes or heroines, or fix them in any other setting than the farm. Would anyone want to hear about cows calving or Jessie tramping the blankets with her bare feet?

At the back of my mind there was always the burning desire, not only to write like Mr Dickens, but to earn enough money to be independent. Not big money, just a sufficiency of coppers to keep me going in sweeties, with maybe a little left over to buy Jessie some hairpins or Jock a twist of his black tobacco. But where could I find such wealth?

While I was still a mixed infant at the village school, I made my first fortune. Fourpence. For 'running with a telegram'.

There was little need to run, for the telegram was of small importance. I knew its contents off by heart. Bella at the post office had told me.

'Will come tomorrow if convenient. Please reply. Signed Chrissie. Stop.'

It was addressed to the minister and I knew fine who Chrissie was. His cousin who lived in a faraway place called Glasgow. Imagine her wanting to leave the fascinations of Sauchiehall Street for a visit to Edgerston Manse! Chrissie, in my opinion, was off her head.

But it was a bonus for me, one that did not often come my way, for few telegrams flew back and forth in the Borders, and when they did Bella had no other means of despatching them than by commandeering anyone who happened to be passing at the time. So I was the lucky one she spotted that morning on my way to school, and called out, 'Will ye rin to the manse wi' a tellygram?'

For fourpence, the rate for the job, I would have run over the Carter Bar. Think of all the caramels and jujubes I could buy. The manse was only a mile away from the post office and I would be passing it anyway on my road to school. So what could be easier?

I clutched the telegram in my hand and ran like the wind, as if the message was of life and death importance. The minister was in his garden, weeding the rockery, when I dashed in through the gate. He looked a trifle startled when I rushed up to him and breathlessly blurted it out.

'Will come tomorrow if convenient. Please reply. Signed Chrissie. Stop.'

He took the telegram, put on his spectacles, and had a close look at it. Then he scribbled a reply, 'Convenient' and handed it back to me.

It might have been convenient for the minister but it put

me off my stride. I had not realized it was a reply-paid telegram and that I would have to go all the way back to the post office with the answer, risking the wrath of Auld Baldy-Heid if I was late for school, as I was sure to be.

It had to be done, so there was nothing else for it but to tear away down the road again, encountering some of my fellow-scholars dawdling on their way up.

'What's wrang?' asked Big Bob, as I went dashing past him. 'Ye're gaun the opposite way.'

'I'm running with a telegram,' I announced, as if I was carrying the Olympic torch.

When I reached the post office I had to do a quick turn round. There was only time to say to Bella, 'Convenient' and ask for a pennyworth of her home-made toffee before I was back on the road again, with a stitch in my side, trying my best to beat the school bell.

But, of course, I was late and had to suffer the consequences. Still, it was worth it, with Bella's toffee to suck and three pennies left in my pocket for future pleasures. I only wished Chrissie would send telegrams more often, but I was never as lucky again.

My only other means of earning money was to cut thistles. My father said he would set me on by the piece, as he did with the Paddies when they were singling turnips. I thought he was pulling my leg, though he seemed serious enough when he handed me a vicious-looking cutter with a long handle, and advised me to use it carefully, suggesting that I make a start on the Lang Field.

Never was there a longer field or one where thistles grew more prolifically. It was like emptying the sea with a teaspoon. The thistles were so tough that they needed several swipes at them before they would budge, and though I worked with a will there seemed more of them in the field when I had finished. But I had some fine blisters on my hands and some scarlet scratches on my legs.

When I went to claim my pay I found that the Boss had

gone off to a lamb sale, taking his wealth with him.

I reminded him when he came home. Fair's fair.

'How many did you cut?' he asked me, as if calculating the rate for the job.

'Thousands .Well, hundreds.'

I was truthful, if nothing else. It was a great handicap.

'Let me see.'

My employer made a play of counting on his fingers and then produced a silver threepenny-piece from his pocket. It was as good as a sovereign to me and I accepted it gratefully. But I realized that if I was ever to make my fortune it was not likely to be in the Lang Field.

I wondered how much Dickens had earned for writing *Oliver Twist* and if he had any blisters on his fingers when he finished. I tried to invent some characters of my own but they all turned out to be animals, with alliterative names, Sandy Squirrel, Willy Weasel, Charlie Crow, Rob Rabbit. And a fish who was later on to swim into the limelight as Tammy Troot.

9. On Four Wheels

It must have been about this time that we took a big plunge
and made our first excursion into foreign territory, not just
over the Border as far as Otterburn, but beyond Newcastle
to the seaside near Whitley Bay: the farthest distance I had
ever travelled in my life, except, of course, to Skyland in my
imagination.

Father – or was it Mother? – had a relative who had made
a mixed marriage and now lived with his English wife at a
place called Cullercoats. Sometimes they came to stay on the
farm, and then I would be relegated to the servant-girl's
bedroom. Now they were returning hospitality, and had
invited us to come and holiday with them. Father was to
drive us there in the motor car.

The Tin Lizzie was a new acquisition and my father had
not yet got the hang of it. Indeed, even when he bought
bigger and better cars as the years went by, he never really
felt at ease with horsepower. Four-legged beasts were more
in his line.

Though it was an exciting prospect, spending a whole fortnight in another country, I had little hopes of arriving there. For one thing, the Boss had no bump of direction. He would turn down any side-road he saw, landing us in dead ends. Often the motor would stick in the mud at the edge of someone's duck-pond. Then we would all have to get out and push before we could get Lizzie back on the road again.

'Ye'd be safer wi' the pownie,' said Jessie, shaking her head dolefully. 'I hae ma doots if ye'll ever mak' it.' She was not the only one.

In order to ease the burden on Lizzie we had packed all our togs into an old trunk, which the hinds had taken by cart in to Jedburgh station to be sent in advance to Cullercoats. It would be waiting for us on arrival. So we thought. In the event, it arrived the day we left, by which time we were all in borrowed raiment and I was wearing somebody's sand-shoes several sizes too big. But we were not to know that on the morning we all packed into the car and the door fell off.

We had to get Jock-the-herd in from the hill, and after a great deal of activity with hammers, screwdrivers and binder-twine, we set off back-firing down the rough farm road.

'I'll keep the kettle on the boil,' called Jessie, as she waved us off. 'Ye'll likely be back.'

But we made it. At least, as far as the main road without any major disaster.

We had our first puncture at the Carter Bar, halfway in England, halfway in Scotland, We could not have chosen a better place if it was scenery we were after.

> Where every prospect pleases,
> And only man is vile.

Looking both ways there were sights to gladden the eye. Catcleuch and Redesdale on the one side and the hills of home on the other, with yellow broom blazing indiscriminately in both countries.

Nearer at hand the picture was not so pleasant. My father was down on his knees wrenching away at the jack, with several of the car's entrails spread out on an old waterproof sheet on the ground – a sight with which I was only too well accustomed whenever we went out on a motoring expedition.

We made it in fits and starts. A puncture was not so bad. Worse trouble came when, miles from a garage, the car gave a splutter and came to a standstill for no apparent reason. Father opened the bonnet and a spout of steam came gushing out. What could be the matter?

'She needs cooling down,' said he, and sent me tramping along the road to the nearest habitation to beg for a kettle of cold water. The lot always fell on Jonah.

My elder brother and sister were with us, home for their holidays from their colleges in Edinburgh, but such menial tasks were not for them. My lady-like sister would never demean herself by begging at doors, and my brother was otherwise occupied, gazing into the mechanism of the engine as if he could cure it by the power of the eye. My mother was sitting by the roadside, patiently prepared to wait for ever, with the baby in her arms, a bouncing youngster by now.

I felt like one of the gypsies who came mooching to the farm for cast-off clothes when I rat-tat-tatted at the nearest door.

'Hullo,' said the child who opened it. Golden ringlets, large blue eyes, a doll tucked under her arm.

'Could your mother lend me some cold water?' I asked. It seemed a silly thing to say.

'Yeth,' she lisped. 'I think tho.' Then she remembered something and her blue eyes grew bigger. 'My mammy'th not in.'

'Oh!' What next?

'My daddy'th here.'

He came to the door in his shirt-sleeves and took command of the situation. Yes, he could provide the water, and brought it out to me in such a large kettle that I could not hold it even with two hands.

'I'll take it,' he said, and closed the door behind him. He went swinging along the road at a great pace, leaving me trotting breathlessly behind him, with the child at my heels, dropping her doll at intervals. By the time I stopped to pick it up and took her by the hand her father was out of sight.

'Come on, we'd better hurry,' I said, urging the child along. But her eyes filled with tears.

'I want a carry,' she wailed, so I had to pick her up, doll and all, and stagger along the road with my burden. Perhaps I would have been better off with the kettle.

When we reached the car, the deed had been done. The motor was ticking over once more, and my father was looking embarrassed, not knowing whether to compensate the man or not. But my mother solved the problem by giving him some fresh eggs which we had brought with us, and he hoisted the child on to his shoulder and went back home.

Once more we packed ourselves into the car and were off.

Beyond Otterburn we were in unknown territory.

'Watch out for signposts,' was the cry.

If there were none at a crossroads, Father with unerring judgement, took the wrong turn and went rattling up to a farm steading, adding miles to the journey. Reversing was one of his weaknesses, and we had to get out and beckon him backwards and forwards.

'A wee bit to the left. Watch out! You'll be in the ditch.'

The greatest problem was how to get through Newcastle without disaster. The town was a confusion of bridges, rivers, docks, and side-streets, many of which Father explored before finally finding the right route.

'Stop blowing the horn,' cried my mother when it

suddenly let out a raucous blast in the middle of the main street; but Father could not stop it, nor could the policeman who rushed forward as if about to arrest the lot of us. Something had seized in the mechanism, so we had to blow our way to the nearest garage, with all the people scuttling out of our path and my lady sister hiding her head in shame.

It was only one of many episodes. Father often said he could write a book, and so he could. I, for one, would have loved to read it, especially if it was written in the pawky way he told the tales of his misadventures on four wheels. It was fun at the time of retelling, not so pleasant if we were involved and had to suffer the tortures of standing shivering by the roadside in wintry weather when the car was stuck in a snowdrift.

Many a time we had to put clanking chains on the wheels, dig ourselves out with spades, and end up as often as not walking home over the slippery roads, leaving Lizzie abandoned by the wayside. I often felt I would have done better on my old baneshaker.

It was late and dark when we finally reached Cullercoats, feeling as if we had circumnavigated the globe. We could not see the sea or anything except some winking lights from the pier and the intermittent flashing of the lighthouse. It was an exciting sight, but I was too tired to take it in.

The discovery that the tin trunk had not arrived meant a hurried consultation about clothes, nightclothes particularly, though I felt that for once I could have slept standing up, and was ready to go to bed in my topcoat if necessary.

The family was to be split up. My parents and the baby were staying at the cousins' small villa. The rest of us were sleeping out at Mrs Somebody's house several streets away. I had a put-up bed in her sitting-room, so narrow and unsteady that I feared it would fold under me and deposit me on the floor. But on that first night I went instantly to sleep in the landlady's pink nightdress and wondered where I was in the morning, with chinks of light coming in through red velvet curtains.

Every morning we went back to the villa to have breakfast with our parents and every evening walked home to our sleeping-quarters. Or, more truthfully, I ran to keep with my brother and sister who crossed streets and disappeared round corners so rapidly that I feared I would get lost and have to spend the night like a ghost wandering through the strange town. Occasionally they called back to me impatiently, 'Hurry up, you! You're a nuisance!' I thought it best to keep out of their way as much as possible during the day.

I had been to the seaside before, at Spittal near Berwick-on-Tweed, and was prepared for the vast ocean but not for the mass of humanity that thronged the beach. There was scarcely a vacant space on the sand, no place where one could just sit quietly and take it all in. As I was accustomed to being on my own for long periods, the constant clamour confused me.

I heard snatches of different dialects. 'Ee! ba goom!' for the first time, as well as the Geordie accent with which I was more familiar. It was my first real taste of communal life. Even when bobbing about in the sea one seemed to be side by side with half the world.

I began to feel as if we had been there for years and could scarcely recall a former existence. I had forgotten what Jessie looked like. I sent her a picture postcard of a fat lady riding a donkey. 'I was on one yesterday', I boasted, but I did not tell her I had fallen off. 'Give my love to Jock.' Love was maybe going a bit too far. I had forgotten what he looked like, too.

I have only muddled memories of that holiday. Deckchairs, donkeys, pierrots, noisy youths playing with a beach ball, a trip to Whitley Bay in a train, and the warm-hearted family from Yorkshire who took me under their wing.

They were always eating out of paper bags and sharing the contents with anyone near by.

''Ave a doughnut, loove.'

Greta, the girl of the family, was like a wild pony. Tawny hair, long legs, and a rough-and-tumble attitude to life. She used to knock me down with an affectionate push and tussle with me on the sand till I cried for mercy. She was as ignorant of Scotland as I was of England, and once asked me if I knew Annie Laurie.

'D'you mean the song?'

'Ee no, loove. I mean her.'

She taught me about Ilkla Moor and I introduced her to the Wee Couper o' Fife. We always ended up in stitches of laughter at our attempts to master each other's language. Still, it was better than struggling with Latin. By the end of the fortnight I felt I belonged to the Kilburn family, and would gladly have gone home with them to their Dales (as indeed they suggested) had it not been for the tug of my own Cheviot hills.

The day came when we had to face the journey home. We all seemed to have expanded in every direction and to have acquired various bulky treasures to take back with us. Shells, smelly seaweed, outsize bars of bright-red rock, and a fuzzy teddy bear which the Kilburns had given me as a parting gift. I was long past the teddy stage so I gave it to the baby who flung it out of the car every time the window was open, adding to the many trials of the journey home.

The tin trunk, having just arrived, had to be taken back again. Father tied it on behind the car, and my task was to look back every now and then, like Lot's wife, to see if it was still there. 'It's loose!' I would call out.

We had so many stoppings and startings one way and another that it was dusky dark by the time we reached the wildest part of the moorland leading up to the Carter Bar, the right moment for the lights to fail.

Father did his best. Indeed, we all gave him advice. What

about pulling out that wee knob? Or turning that screw? Maybe that loose wire has something to do with it.

He tried everything, but without any result. So in the end there was nothing else for it but to park at the roadside and wait for the daylight, taking turns to act as look-out for approaching vehicles who might run into us.

We had no torch, so we struck matches when we heard a car coming, waving them in the air like will o' the wisps. The traffic was few and far between, and no one stopped to ask about our plight. Only a tramp shuffling by inquired if he could have a fill of tobacco for his empty pipe. My father gave it to him, as well as something from his pocket, and I broke off a piece of Cullercoats rock to help him on his way.

Now and again we dozed off in the back of the car or wandered about in the eerie darkness. Gradually a faint glow showed in the sky and soon the birds began to twitter their morning song. When we could see a few hundred yards ahead, Father said, 'I think I'll crank her up now. It's safe to go.'

The hinds were on their way to the work-stable when we came rattling up the home stretch. It was comforting to know that Jessie would be in the kitchen with the kettle boiling, and that we were safely back in our ain countree. Tin Lizzie would be put to rest next to the gig in the cart-shed. It was great to get rid of her.

As days went by a variety of strange equipages found their way up the farm road. The homely horse and cart was still to the fore, but some adventurous souls had branched out into motor-bicycles and sidecars. They dressed up in goggles, large leather gloves and coats, with the passenger, tucked into the sidecar, swathed in shawls and scarves. They were usually stiff with cold when they emerged, and declared that our road had 'rattled their internals' till everything was out of place.

Once in a while an enormous lorry came rolling up the road laden with sacks containing a mysterious concoction called guano. The men unloaded the sacks and later spread the contents on the fields, like a sprinkling of snow.

'What is it?' I asked them.

'Och! it's just birds' droppings,' said Tam. 'Guid for the grund.'

Certainly it looked more pleasant than the dung which the hinds usually spread on the fields, and had a less 'healthy' smell.

The largest vehicle which ever negotiated our rough road was the mill, which came out from Jedburgh once a year after harvest-time to convert the sheaves into corn. It was like a puffing Billy, all steam and loud shuddering noises. Even the proud bubblyjock went and hid to keep out of its way.

For some reason, the mill required a constant supply of water to keep it shuddering and shaking. Anyone with strong enough arms was sent with pails to the water-barrel or to the kitchen taps to slake its thirst while it was regurgitating the sheaves. I was afraid to go near it, like the bubblyjock, for it belched out so much smoke that it blinded me. And there was always the fear that it might draw me into its clutches, mistaking me for one of the sheaves.

The hinds fed its hungry maw with the ripe sheaves, while my father waited anxiously to test the quality of the corn that came trickling out. He gathered a sample of it into a little bag to be shown later to the corn-merchant. The men shovelled it into sacks and forked the chaff into a corner of the straw-barn. The kaff-hole, it was called, a dark place which I dreaded when hunting for eggs. I knew there would be some there, but there was always the danger of a rat lurking amongst the chaff or a hen flying out in my face.

On the whole I preferred the horse-driven traffic, the gigs, the baker's van, and our own carts pulled by the Clydesdales.

We had not yet come round to the idea of a tractor, though the Boss was considering it. So the hinds told me one day when I was in the work-stable at lowsing-time.

'Damned nonsense!' grumbled Wull, using the curry-comb on Prince's sleek coat. 'Your faither'll hae us fleein' aboot in airyplanes next. Gie me a horse ony time.'

'That's so,' agreed Tam, lighting his pipe. 'Horses is human, an' what's mair, *they* never break doon.'

10. Growth

By now I seemed to have lived for centuries and sometimes
said to Jessie, as if I was a weary woman of the world,
'D'you remember away back in the old days when I was
young . . . ?'

But I was still not too old to be shut in the household jail
as a punishment, and spent many a long hour in the garret
in solitary confinement.

It was a great place for contemplation, not for thinking
over my sins – I was always unjustly imprisoned, in my
opinion – but for dreaming up a story or wondering why
I was here. Not in the garret, but in the universe. If God took
care of every sparrow that flew and every blade of grass that
grew, what I wondered did He make of me? He must have
some plan in His head? I pictured Him sitting up there turning over the pages of a golden jotter till He came to my name.
Did He shake His head and sigh, like Jessie?

'That lassie! What'll I mak' o' her? She's got nae rummlegumption.'

But, of course, God would not speak in a Border accent, would He?

There were many things to puzzle about, crime and punishment for example. It was always for doing good deeds that I was sent to jail. I was a great giver-away, especially of other folks' belongings, and when a gypsy woman came to the door one day whining that her man had 'nae soles to his shoon', what could be kinder than to give her a pair of my father's?

They were old brown ones, and I thought he would never miss them. But, of course, he did, and I had to pay the penalty.

The worst of being in prison was that my jailors never indicated the length of my sentence, and often forgot that I was still there. Setting me free depended on when it came up their backs, if they were passing by the garret door, or if they heard me calling, 'Let me out! *Ouvrez la porte!*'

I remember that particular day because it grew dark so early and there was nothing to be seen except the faintest glow from the moon shining in through the skylight window.

During daylight there was always plenty to do in the garret, old books to read, a rocking-horse to ride, the contents of a large wooden chest to explore. It was full of feather boas and other discarded finery, a great place in which to rummage when looking for garments to clothe a new tattie-bogle. It was bitterly cold in the garret so I often dressed myself up as well, in old shawls, beaded dolmans, or a moth-eaten fur cape.

On that day I felt I had been abandoned when I heard the Tin Lizzie being cranked up. Were my parents going out for the evening leaving me to my fate? By the time I had climbed on to the rickety washstand and propped up the skylight window, the car was puttering away down the road. I could see Jessie disappearing, too, into the darkness on her way home to the herd's cottage. There would be no one left in the house except the sleeping baby and a servant-lassie miles away down in the kitchen. The Cairthorse, I think it was.

I pictured her sitting drowsing by the cosy kitchen fire with her slippered feet on the fender, or maybe trying to pen a letter to her lad, Gorge. She would never be thinking of me. Nobody seemed to miss me when I was out of sight, I was so used to going my own way.

No amount of rattling at the door or calling for help would attract her attention at that distance. There was nothing for it but to wait till she came upstairs to bed. The garret, friendly enough in the daytime, was now full of frightening shadows. I could hear strange creaks and rustles, the scampering of mice on the skirting-boards, the eerie hooting of an owl from the roof. Everything took on fantastic shapes. Even the old rocking-horse seemed to be moving, and the dressmaker's dummy in the corner was swaying from side to side, as if she had come to life.

The only consolation I had was in thinking of the remorse my parents would feel when they found my corpse stiff and cold, stretched out on the garret floor.

'Dead, dead! beyond recall. . . .'

I visualized my own funeral and heard the minister in a broken voice, proclaiming my virtues. Never speak ill of the dead. All my shortcomings would be forgotten. Never had there been such a bright beautiful biddable child. What a loss to her sorrowing family, one that could never be replaced.

I looked down from Paradise on my heartbroken parents and decided to forgive them, but not for a while. Let them suffer first. Serve them right.

At last a step on the stairs. The Cairthorse lumbering on her way to bed, carrying her candle and her stone hot-water bottle. The pig.

I left the pearly gates and hurried to the garret door, calling, 'Let me *out*! Open the *door*!' No use *ouvrezing la porte* for her.

Liz-Ann almost dropped the pig, but at least she heard me and had the sense to set me free.

'Mercy goodness! I thought ye were a ghost,' said she, as white as a sheet.

'Well, I'm not,' I said crossly, and ran past her down to the kitchen to warm myself at the dying embers of the fire.

The clothes-horse was standing there – the winter-dyke – airing its load of clean washing. Jessie had been doing the ironing and goffering earlier that day, using the old box iron with its three-cornered stones which she heated in the depths of the fire till they were red hot. There was a hole in the corner of the stones through which she pushed the poker when she wanted to retrieve one. It was a perilous performance, conveying it, sizzling with heat to the iron which she held in one hand, open at the end to receive it, and a great relief when it was finally shut in. I was always terrified she might drop it on the cat.

Not Jessie. All her actions were co-ordinated, unlike the servant-girl with her fumbling fingers and two left feet. Jessie had an economy of movement and a steady pace, never dashing at things or getting into a fankle. All the fairies must have been at her christening, for she even had the gift of green fingers, and when she had nothing better to do in the house she would go out into the garden with a trowel in her hand.

'Come on, wumman,' she would say to a drooping dahlia. 'Stand up an' show some smeddum.'

Ten to one the dahlia would respond, and before long would be standing upright straightening out its petals. I felt Jessie could have given a lesson or two to Mrs Pot Plant.

Country gardens on the whole were hitty-missy affairs, not plotted and planned but left to grow wild, with nettles and weeds mixed up with the flowers. Most farmers had too much to do with sowing and growing during their working hours to bother about cultivating finicky little patches around their houses in their spare time. Why waste hours weeding a small garden when a whole field of thistles was awaiting their attention?

Often it was left to their women folk to attend to the garden but they, too, had little enough time to spend on such a task, with the result that many farmhouses had nothing to show in the way of flowers at their doors other than a few rambler roses, a sturdy bush or two, and some clumps of candytuft. Anything that grew without needing constant attention.

Not so, in our case. My father and mother were keen gardeners. In theory, that is. Mother took turns and Father was constant in his fondness of growing sweet peas. But it was a hunger or a burst.

As for gardens we had not one but four, the front garden, the side garden, the back garden, and the top garden. The top garden was the biggest of all, across the road and some distance away from the house, where there were masses of berry-bushes, rows and rows of vegetables, my father's sweet peas, and the greenhouse in which he often took refuge.

It was his hidey-hole, a place where he could escape from family bothers and retreat when he wanted to pursue some ploy of his own. Not just planting out seedlings, but prac- tising a comic song, playing the fiddle, or puzzling over unpaid accounts. He kept an overflow of odds and ends in the greenhouse: old newspapers, unanswered letters, sheet- music, false moustaches and wigs which he used when doing a funny turn at local concerts, his old fiddle, and a little notebook in which he jotted down goodness knows what. His chaotic accounts perhaps.

'Where's the Boss? Away and fetch him.'

When I was given this order I always knew where to find him, but I hated being the one to disturb his peace. I was all for secret withdrawals myself and knew how I would resent being jerked back to reality if I was in the middle of a reverie. Sometimes I could see him through the glass panes gesturing away to an unseen audience. Or maybe he would have his spectacles on, studying a seed packet.

Would it be better to knock at the door or throw a handful of pebbles at the glass windows to warn him of my approach?

'You're wanted,' I mouthed, if he turned and saw me. But I never went in. It was his castle, and I had mine on the hill. Privacy was precious.

Father was not always in the greenhouse. Often I found him pottering amongst his precious sweet peas, training them up in the way they should go, nipping off dead buds or just standing admiring their delicate colourings. He was known in the district as an expert and always won first prize, not only at the local show but at the big one in Jedburgh, held in the town hall and with all the county competing.

Every year there was a special prize for the best decorated table. A flower-arrangement. It was the women folk who did the decorating, with the men standing by giving advice. There was as much tension in the air as if they were competing for a crown.

When the day came my mother was 'up to high Doh', having to bear such a burden of responsibility on her shoulders. Father had been in the garden at the crack of dawn, gathering his best blooms and deciding which shades would look best. A mixture of pale blues and pinks? Or dark blues and salmon? Or just pinks alone with trails of gypsophila in between?

It was a difficult decision to make. In the end he took bunches of all kinds and colours, and waited to see the effect when Mother had set to work in the town hall.

I had a humble hand in the proceedings, for it was not only the flowers that were being judged but the general layout of the table. Various appurtenances had to be brought out and cleaned, in particular the silvery epergne which we used on the dining-room table on the rare occasions when we wanted to impress visitors.

It was a perfect nuisance, in my opinion, as it was made up of complicated bits and pieces which had to be fitted together, as well as cleaned and polished. Apart from the ornamental centre-piece, there were four little gates to be set at each corner of the table, also to be filled with flowers. And though the final effect, with airy-fairy gypsophila trailing in between, was pleasing to the eye, I agreed with Jessie when she said, 'Gie me a plain vawse ony day. It's less palaver.'

Her task was to produce a sparklingly white tablecloth stiff with starch. So in the end we all felt a stab of pride when our combined efforts resulted once more in another win for Overton Bush. But it was really Father who had done the deed with his sweet peas.

I remember when Mother decided to make a rockery in the side garden, to fill up an ugly corner, and set us all to work building a base of large stones, cast-off kettles, broken tubs, handleless pails, old crockery. Anything and everything went into it. We tried to cover them all with soil, but if a downpour came, the rain washed it all away and we could see a kettle spout or an old teapot coming to the surface. It would have been less bother to build the Pyramids.

Livestock, too, would get into the garden, no matter how hard we tried to keep the gate shut. Grumphy liked nothing better than routing in the rockery, and did his best to knock the whole edifice down, cocks and hens scratched up the soil, dogs buried their bones there, and the bubblyjock pecked at the plants.

But in the end Mother succeeded. The wilderness was not entirely transformed, but at least she could see results for her labours when flowers began to flourish in between the stones and old teapots. I was never sure of their names. They were just blue flowers or pink ones. Indeed, I was not certain which were weeds, and wondered why a dandelion, for example, should rate lower than a primula. They were both flowers, were they not?

My own efforts never came to much. I had been given a small patch in the back garden around a gnarled old apple tree, which must have been blighted judging by the few wizened apples it produced. The soil seemed sour, for nothing I planted would flourish, even though I begged some guano from the hinds to sprinkle on it. But maybe it was my fault, for I always expected seeds to sprout instantly and plants to take root even when I had dug up primroses, forget-me-nots, and marshmarigolds from the banks of the burn. Poor things, they must have felt homesick, for they soon shrivelled and died. My one success was a bush of southernwood. Appleringie, Jessie called it.

Once a year the laird's garden at the Big Hoose was thrown open to the public, and we would walk sedately along the well-kept paths and admire the formal layout. It was all too precise for my liking, with every flower standing to attention and not a weed to be seen.

I preferred the higgledy-piggledy arrangement of my granny's cottage garden at Camptown, and spent many happy hours pottering about amongst her peony-roses and rasp-bushes. She did not mind the odd wild flower or bishop-weed, or even dandelion. I had more success there than in my own unproductive plot at home. The butterflies and bumblebees, too, seemed to prefer the mixed scents in Granny's garden.

One day we were ordered by the art master at the Grammar School to bring in a bunch of flowers to draw. Fancy having an art master! Auld Baldy-Heid never bothered with such a subject. The only thing I drew at the village school was a cow on the blackboard, and not a very convincing one at that. Now we had to think of backgrounds, perspectives, and still life. We had already tried out our talents on an apple, an orange, and a vase. We were now to progress to higher things. Flowers.

I wondered if I could mooch some sweet peas from my father, but, remembering I would have to draw them, I settled for something simpler, a bunch of gowans from the meadow.

I got up early to gather them in the morning dew, and they looked fresh enough when I started out, but by the time I reached the road-end they had already begun to wilt.

Black Sandy took one as he hoisted me on to the bus. 'Tooral-ooral-addy!' he roared, sticking the flower into his lapel. Then he began to sing 'Auld Lang Syne' at the pitch of his voice.

> 'We twa hae run aboot the braes
> An' pou'd the gowans fine. . . .'

When we arrived at the school gates I had only one solitary flower left intact, which I had managed to rescue from the boisterous onslaughts of my fellow-passengers. I stuck it in my pocket for safety and dreaded the moment when I would have to bring it out to show to the art master. He was a nice enough man, but his tongue was sarcastic, and I knew I would be walking right into his trap.

'What's this?' he asked, peering at my crumpled offering.

'It's a g-gowan,' I gulped.

'You mean it was a gowan,' he said, throwing it into the waste-paper basket. 'Don't you grow any decent flowers out in the wilds? Perhaps I should have asked you to bring in a pig. Here!' He thrust a rose into my hand, from a bunch which one of the town scholars had brought in. A beautiful scarlet, scented bloom. '*That's* what a flower should be like. Go ahead and draw it.'

But I didn't. I drew the gowan instead. Or, at least, I tried to. Anybody, I argued to myself, could draw an upright rose. A wilting gowan called for much more artistic skill.

It was a pity I had none. After taking one look at my offering, the art master tore it up and pitched it into the wastepaper basket to keep the gowan company.

'There's one thing you'll never be,' he told me darkly, 'and that's an artist.'

11. Visitors and Visiting

One day Bella Confectionery from the post office rang up.

'Have ye heard the latest?'

'No, not yet,' I replied, all agog.

It was not often I got the chance of answering the telephone myself, but I happened to be alone in the house at the time except for Jessie who would sooner have had all her teeth drawn than speak into 'thon noisy beast'. Mother was busy at her rockery and Father was shut up in the greenhouse. Bella was a trifle disappointed when she found she had no better ears than mine to fill, but she drew a deep breath and made the most of it.

'Wait till I tell ye! Ye ken the minister?'

'Yes, fine.'

'Well, ye'll never guess!'

'Mercy me! what's happened?' I had visions of him confiscating the contents of the kirk plate or running away with the organist.

'Fell aff his byke. Right fornent ma door.'

'Goodness gracious! Is he dead?'

'Nut at all!' This was going a little too far. 'Bumped his heid. I've just put a bandage on't. But ye should see his byke. Ruined. The baker's given him a lift hame in his cairt, but I doot if he'll manage to preach on Sunday.'

'But the baker never preaches. . . . Oh, I see, you mean the minister. Oh well, maybe we'll get a holiday,' I said hopefully.

'Nut at all! They'll likely get a locum.'

'A what?'

Bella clicked her teeth impatiently. I could tell she was not enjoying the conversation as much as she had anticipated.

'Are ye sure there's naebody else in? A'weel, ye'll pass on the news? Ta-ta, lassie.'

As it turned out, the minister was less damaged than his bicycle and was able to preach on Sunday with a black eye and a bandage on his brow. It was something to look at during the long sermon, and the drama of the affair kept Bella going for weeks.

She was our lifeline for, apart from passing on gossip, Bella acted as a warning system.

'That's the Scotts awa' by. They'll likely be on their way to veesit ye. The hale jing-bang's in the buggy. Ye'd better get the kettle on.'

Not only the kettle. Her advance warning gave us time to put on the girdle as well, to bake a batch of scones and pancakes, so that thanks to Bella we were able to feed the hungry visitors when they arrived 'unexpectedly' in the buggy.

When we were storm-stayed in winter, what we missed most during the snow-siege was Bella's chatty voice on the telephone when the line went dead. Even Jessie rejoiced at the sound of thon noisy beast when the thaw came and we heard the first ring, followed by Bella telling us, 'That's you back on the line. Are ye a' richt up there? Have ye heard the latest? Mrs Broon's chimney went on fire, Mary-Anne's got the mumps, an' the Mains's coo's calved. . . .'

It was like music to our ears.

Sometimes, in spite of Bella's vigilance and the fact that the farm led to nowhere but the great beyond, we had the odd unexpected visitor who had strayed off the beaten track. It was exciting to see an unknown carriage or car coming up the road and to speculate on who could be coming to call.

I remember a strange man arriving one day at the front door, wearing plus-fours and asking, 'Can you show me the way to the golf course?'

'The what?' I asked, stupefied.

Father and Mother were away on their weekly visit to the other farm, Swinside Townhead, and once more I was the only one at home. It would be a tale to tell them when they came back, but they would likely not believe me.

'The golf course,' repeated the man impatiently. He looked at me as if I was the village idiot. 'Don't tell me there isn't one, after I've driven all the way up this terrible road. I've seen people playing somewhere up here when I was motoring by on the main road. So I thought, seeing I had my clubs with me today, I might fit in a round or two. Where is it?'

'Oh, that!' I said, beginning to understand. 'Well, you see, it's not really a golf course. . . .'

How could I explain that Father, who had a selection of broken-down mashies and niblicks, sometimes took a few golf balls out on to the hill and swiped his way round an imaginary course? He had made little holes on the 'greens' but the balls seldom went into them, disappearing instead down rabbit-holes, never to be seen again. So many, indeed, went to ground that he used to say a rubber plantation would spring up on the hill one day in the future.

It was a hazardous course, full of ups and downs. Father had appropriate names for the different holes: The Himalayas, Crossing the Styx, The Slough of Despond, Danger Ahead. Apart from divots, bracken and rabbit-holes, there was always the problem of beasts. The sheep refused to get out of the way, and it was no use shouting 'Fore!' to the bull.

I tried to explain all this to the stranger but he still insisted that he wanted to play, and was about to get his gear out of the car when I gave him my parting shot.

'The bull's there. He's awful wild.'

That did it. Without another word he got into the car, hastily reversed it and shot away down the road.

'Guid riddance,' said Jessie who had been watching from the kitchen window. 'They'll be comin' speirin' for the circus next.' As if we had hundreds and thousands of strangers beating a path to our door.

Friendly droppers-in were always welcome, whether Bella had warned us of their approach or not, and were invited to take pot luck at the kitchen table if we were having a plain meal instead of a fancy one. But if they came by special invitation they were assured of a big spread in the dining-room with a vase of flowers gracing the centre of the table, if not the epergne. Even in autumn and winter we had rowan berries or holly, and Christmas roses as pale as porcelain. Mother had not served her apprenticeship at the flower show for nothing.

When we were invited out as a family I was warned not to eat too much or ask for a second helping, which I thought strange since Mother was always pressing second and third helpings on the folk who visited us.

'Pass in your cup for some more tea, and you'll take another slice of cake? Oh nonsense! you've eaten nothing. Try another wee bit.' But it did not seem to work the other way round.

Other folk's food, of course, always tasted better. It was the difference that did it. Even seeing it served on other dishes with unfamiliar patterns on them somehow sharpened the appetite. I wondered if castor-oil might not taste so terrible out of a crystal goblet, but I had my doubts about that.

Though we lived well enough at home it was not always easy to vary the menu. Being so far from shops we had to eat what was available. It was a treat when we could get tasty kippers, or herring fried in a covering of oatmeal; and though there was no shortage of game, I thought sausages the rarest of foods and far more succulent than grouse.

Looking back, I marvel at the variety of puddings mother and Jessie managed to concoct. Not 'sweets'. Good wholesome stick-to-the-ribs puds. Clooty dumplings, so called because they were boiled in a clout – the Scottish word for a cloth – roly-poly puddings, treacle and syrup sponges, apple dumplings, Bakewell tarts, and a variety of fruit pies. They were not just afters, they were a meal in themselves, especially when topped with plenty of fresh cream.

'Ye dinna ken what's guid for ye,' Jessie would scold if I left some on my plate. 'Och weel! it's no' lost what a freend'll get,' she said when she tipped it into the pigs' pail.

The cottage wives seldom saw the inside of a shop and had to rely on Wattie, who came once a week in his horse-driven van with a variety of goods to sell. It was scarcely a supermarket, but to country eyes it contained treasure-trove. Fresh pan loaves, meat pies, cream cookies, flour, sugar, boiled sweets, paraffin oil, bootlaces, scrubbing-brushes. There were shelves in the back which Wattie drew out to display his goods while the wives stood by with their purses in their hands and their aprons gathered up ready to receive their purchases.

Like the postie, Wattie obliged by doing messages in the town. He took clogs to the cobbler, collected sheep-dip, and sometimes brought a selection of blouses for the wives to try on. Many a Sunday hat had journeyed out the Jed in Wattie's van.

'There's a broon felt an' a black straw. Tak' your pick.'

It was little wonder we all waited so eagerly for the road to be cleared after a snowstorm. Wattie's visit was the highlight of the week.

His horse, whom Wattie just called 'Horse', must have been a very tough beast. He pulled the creaky van the long miles from town, and went all over the district, struggling up farm roads even rougher than ours to visit outlying cottagers. When he arrived at our door, Horse almost sat down with relief, sensing he could have a long rest and a nibble in his nosebag while Wattie came into the house for a cup of tea.

'Bide there an' dinna budge, Horse,' Wattie told him before coming into the kitchen and sinking down in the nearest chair. 'I'll just rest ma shanks for twa-three meenits,' said he, loosening his bootlaces.

The twa-three meenits were sometimes elongated, depending on the state of Wattie's shanks and how long it took him to drink his tea. It was no ordinary operation, for Wattie had a walrus moustache, and Jessie served him his tea in a moustache-cup. I was always fascinated by the precedure. Wattie swept up his bristles so that his lips were clear before taking a one-sided swill from the cup. Then out came his red spotted handkerchief to mop his moustache after every mouthful. It would have been easier, I thought, to trim off all that hair, but Wattie would not have been Wattie without it.

'I'll need to be on the go,' he sighed when he had tied up his bootlaces; but not before he had turned every penny he could, for Wattie was something of a Shylock, a great buyer and seller, with as many sidelines as a railway junction. He was always on the look-out for fresh eggs, butter, cheese, sacks of potatoes or garden produce which he could buy in the country and sell at a profit in the town.

He drove a hard bargain down to the smallest farthing, and noted each transaction in a bulging notebook, sucking the point of his pencil through his drooping moustache.

When settling-up time came there was a great hunting around for small change, and many a calculation had to be done while Wattie deducted the cost of cookies, loaves, syrup and Abernethy biscuits from the price he was offering for eggs and butter. He had a leather pouch jingling with coins from which he carefully extracted the odd pennies before tying it up again and replacing it in a secret pocket in the inside of his jacket. The heavier it became the broader Wattie beamed as he went back to his van.

'Come on, Horse, we'll need to be gettin' doon the road.' And that was the end of Wattie for another week.

Apart from his visit and that of the postie we had little to hope for unless the hunt rode by in full fling or a gypsy caravan came creaking up the road. But once in a while a miracle happened and a new set of human beings arrived, not just for a day but to live on the farm.

There was little chopping and changing amongst the workers, but I remember the excitement when one year a new hind and his family arrived at term-time.

Every year, long before the term, Father went through the motions of 'speaking to the men', asking them if they meant to stay on. Or, indeed, sacking them if they were unsatisfactory workers, though this seldom happened. If they indicated that they were content, all was well. If not, it behoved the Boss to stand in the market-place in Jedburgh on hiring day and find replacements from the farm-workers who gathered there in search of employment.

I was never sure how this worked or how a bargain was struck. It seemed to be done so casually, by word of mouth. No signing or sealing. Yet I never heard of anyone going back on his word.

The wives in question did not set eyes on their new home till the day of the flitting. The hind himself came in advance on his bicycle for an odd Saturday afternoon for the purpose of setting the garden. He would dig over the soil, plant potatoes and turnips, set rows of seeds, and hope that everything would be sprouting by the time he came to take possession.

On the day of the flitting there were great comings and goings, for the one cottager had to get out with all his belongings before the other could come in. Father sent men with empty carts to the farm which the new hind was leaving, while strange carts arrived at the cottage door to take away the furniture of the departing family.

All day long they carried out chairs, tables, grandfather clocks, crockery and bedding. Everyone prayed for 'a guid day for the flittin'', for it was a pitiful process trying to pack the carts in pouring rain and to fit everything under waterproof covers. Sad, too, to see the familiar nick-nacks disappearing from sight for ever: the china dogs, the aspidistra, the jelly-pan, the family Bible. But there was little time for sentimental goodbyes. The out-goers had to be smartly on their way to reach their new abode before the darkening, often passing their opposite numbers on the road.

The fires were kept going in the empty house, and Jessie saw that there was food and milk left there to await the arrival of the weary travellers. It would be late that night before they got to bed, for the carts had to be unloaded before the flitters could finally settle in. But at least there would be a kettle on the boil to welcome them.

I remember watching the carts coming rumbling up the road in the gloaming, and wondering what household treasures lay under the tarpaulin covers. There might be livestock, too, a piglet, perhaps, a few hens, or a bantam cockerel.

Jock-the-herd used to tell me of a family who flitted so regularly every year that when term day came round the bantam lay down on the rug and held up its legs to be tied; but I knew it was just one of Jock's tales.

In the morning there would be different curtains on the windows, different patterns of pipe-clay on the doorstep, and a new Mrs Thing shaking her rug. The most interesting thing for me to find out was if there were any children in the family who might play with me, or allow me to boss them, if they were small enough. I could show off my superior knowledge to impress them.

'You don't know what a triangle is? Oh well, I'll tell you.' Poor things!

As it turned out, there was a gaggle of them, all looking more or less alike. I called them Eeny, Meenie, Miny and Mo till I got their names sorted out. I liked Mo best, for she was only a toddler and thought I was perfect. There was another on the way, so the new Mrs Thing had little time to shake rag rugs or gossip on the doorstep. But she seemed contented enough, for I sometimes heard her singing as I passed by.

> 'O can ye sew cushions,
> Can ye sew sheets,
> Can ye sing Ba-loo-loo
> When the bairnie greets?'

12. Trials and Tribulations

'This has been the worst day of my life,' I announced to Jessie when I reached home one snowy evening, chittering with cold and my hair frozen into icicles.

Jessie's reply was characteristic. 'Hoots, lassie, ye're no' feenished wi' life. Ye'll hae mony a worse day, if ye live lang enough.'

It was cold comfort on such a freezing day, but at the same time she was taking practical steps to thaw me out by divesting me of my outer garments, dishing up a bowl of hot soup and keeping me at a safe distance from the direct heat of the fire, 'in case ye come oot in chilblains'.

It was not only the bitter cold that had troubled me that day, though that was bad enough, eating as it did into my bones and chilling my very marrow. There were other forces working against me, as if all the gremlins in the world had taken a scunner at me. I tried to tell Jessie about it, but nothing ever sounded the same in the retelling. Either I understated the turn of events or exaggerated them. It was the same when I tried to write things down. Maybe Charles Dickens, with his sharper pen, could have made a better job of it.

It began in the raw darkness of the early morning.

> In winter I get up at night
> And dress by yellow candle-light.

I felt like a pit pony or one of the moles Jessie used to tell me about, the moudiwarts who lived underground and seldom saw the light of day. It was dark when I set off to school in the morning and pitch black by the time I reached home again. But the worst part was getting up in the icy-cold bedroom, with the windows frosted over and the hot-water bottle stone cold, knowing that I would be forced to go out into the even icier atmosphere that awaited me beyond the shelter of the farmhouse walls.

The trouble about being a scholar at the Grammar School was that, unlike Auld Baldy-Heid's institution, it never closed when there was a storm. The main road to Jedburgh was kept open by snowplough, and I was expected to struggle down to the road-end as best I could to board Black Sandy's bus, often up to the armpits in snow-wreaths.

No excuses. Archie-Bald, the rector, had a heavy hand with truants. There were deadly exams looming up, and all dolts and dunces were expected to attend every lesson, frozen stiff or not. Easy enough for him, living in a house cheek by jowl with the school. He could leave his warm fireside five minutes before the bell rang, with no pitying thought to spare for country pupils who had to get up hours before in the cold dawn.

Nothing could be bleaker than that walk over the snowy wastes in the early morning, with the chill air finding every chink in my armour. Even though I was well wrapped up, with a long woollen scarf – a gravat – tied over my head and round my neck, I was soon shivering. There was no chance of walking smartly to keep the circulation going.

Every step was hazardous, slipping and sliding without making much progress. And there was no telling whether I was on the road or the hillside, everything was so blocked up. Only the tops of some snow-laden trees helped to give me my bearings.

Time and again I fell into a snow-filled ditch and had to haul myself out. By now my fingers were so frozen that I had no feeling in them and could scarcely carry my school bag. All the time I thought of the day's lessons awaiting me and the poem I had to learn off by heart.

> I chatter, chatter as I flow
> To join the brimming river.
> For men may come and men may go
> But I go on for ever.

It did not apply to our burn at home which was lost beneath the snow, nor to the river Jed which lay silent and unchattering under the frozen ice.

At last I reached the road-end and saw the bus waiting for me. Black Sandy was out on the road, flapping his arms and stamping his feet to keep warm. Usually I was there in good time but he always gave me a few minutes' grace in snowy weather.

'Come on, wee ane. Speed up. Jings! ye look like a frosted tattie. Hop in.'

The cold had done little to curb Black Sandy's spirits. He sang louder, if anything, as we rattled in the Jed road. Rattled was the word, for Sandy had put clanking chains on his tyres, which made a raucous din every time they spun round. Even so, they did not drown his song.

> 'There ance was a very pawky duke
> Far-kent for his joukery-pawkery.
> He owned a hoose wi' a grand ootlook,
> A gairden an' a rockery.

Hech mon! The pawky duke!
Hoot ay! An' a rockery!
For a bonnet laird wi' a sma' kailyaird
Is naethin' but a mockery.'

Sandy went on for verse after verse, stopping when he had to collect another shivering young passenger by the wayside and picking up again where he had left off.

'His nose was red as ony rose,
His legs were lang an' bony. . . .'

Indeed, all our noses were redder than roses by the time we reached the town, for we had to get out so often to heave the bus forward when it skidded or stuck in a snow-drift. I was terrified the worst would happen and the school gates would be closed against us when we got there, with the fearsome Janny glowering at us through the railings. But Black Sandy did his best to make up for lost time by riding his charger at full speed when the going was good, and tooted his horn in triumph when he swung into the High Street.

We made it. The bell was giving its final clang when we shuddered to a standstill outside the gates.

'Oot ye get!' roared Black Sandy. 'Ye're just in time. Onward Christian Soldiers!'

In we trooped and the prison gates were shut behind us. I thought there was a disappointed gleam in the janitor's eye. Little did I realize I would see that gleam again later in the day when my blackest nightmare came true.

Miss Crichton's catarrh was worse that day. She spent a great deal of time blowing on her handkies and drying them off on the radiator. It seemed an unhygienic practice, but who were we to complain? Soon we were all steaming, as our wet garments began to dry off in the comparative warmth of the classroom. Before long I had a swimmy feeling in my head and a great desire to lay it down on the desk. It was difficult to concentrate on lessons, but we were forced to remain alert, for, busy though she was with her handkerchiefs, Miss Crichton was determined to put us through our paces, with the impending examinations in mind.

We all had to say '*Bonjour, mam'selle*' to her and answer her questions in French, an impossible task for me. I had not yet sorted out the males from the females, and was rapped smartly over the knuckles for referring to my book as *une livre* and to my seat as *un chaise*.

'*Tu es une* idiot,' she ranted to me in her North-East accent. '*Une* silly idiot!'

I felt sillier as the lessons went on. Strange what a word of praise can do or alternatively a word of blame. If one is designated a donkey one does one's best to bray. By the time I reached the English class, where I could usually hold my own, I could not remember without constant promptings the verses I was supposed to repeat. The poem sounded idiotic, intoned in my broad Border tongue.

> 'I slip, I slide, I gloom, I glance
> Among my skimming swallows.
> I make the netted sunbeams dance
> Against my sandy shallows.'

I could not blame the other pupils for giggling behind my back. It was not done out of malice, it was just something to break the monotony. For were they not all my friends by now? This revelation had completely overwhelmed me, coming as it did out of the blue.

It had happened during the time I was forced to stay off for a whole fortnight with a 'fever', bad enough to necessitate a visit from the doctor. He came smelling of antiseptic, in his chauffeur-driven car, and after sounding me with his stethoscope, took my temperature and left instructions that I was to lie still and take light nourishment.

There had been a great to-do in anticipation of his visit,

with the bedroom fire lit for his benefit and a tray set out with the best china and a lace cloth in case he fancied a cup of tea. I felt guilty at causing such a stir and making my mother dress up in her best frock in the middle of the morning. Father, too, could not settle to anything till the great man had come and gone, for the visit always ended in the parlour with the doctor receiving some stronger refreshment than that on the tea-tray.

Lying still and taking light nourishment no doubt helped to reduce the fever though it made me feel like a trapped animal at the zoo. Jessie or the servant-girl brought the food up on a tin tray – no fancy lace cloths for me – dumped it down on the rickety bedside table and said, 'Here ye are. Eat every bite, or else!'

Thin gruel, lightly boiled eggs mushed up with bread in a cup, beef tea and tapioca pudding did little to tempt my appetite, but it was not the eating that mattered to me. I would sooner have had a gulp of fresh air, and felt sure I could have cured myself faster if I had been left up a tree rather than in a stuffy bedroom.

Lack of reading material added to the dreariness of the long days. I had devoured everything from *Oliver Twist* (twice) to the text on the wall calender and the stock market in the *Scotsman*, and was almost reduced to my Latin grammar when the Cairthorse came stumping upstairs after the postie had called.

'Here's a letter for ye.'

'Never!'

My temperature shot sky-high when I saw that it was indeed addressed to me with a Jedburgh postmark. Inside was a get well card with a picture of an elephant on it (not forgotten), signed by every single one of my classmates and with an added message: 'Come back soon, we're missing you.'

Fancy that!

I could not have been more surprised if Dafty had sent

his love to me or the great Miss Crichton herself had written, '*Je suis* absolutely lost *sans toi*.'

I could hardly wait to get back, though I felt a little embarrassed when I came face to face with them again; but I need not have bothered, for they showed no outward signs of affection. All the same, I felt it was there. They still pulled my leg mercilessly and laughed at my accent, but there was no malice in it. I was no longer just an oddity, I was one of them.

But it did not help me much with 'The Brook'. Even the mild English teacher had succumbed to Miss Crichton's temper and to her cold.

'Sid dowd, you're hopeless,' she told me between sneezes. 'You'll have to begid at the begidding and leard it all over agaid. Atishoo!'

By the time we were let out for the lunch break I felt that many a long year had passed, and the day was still far from done. Indeed, the first lesson in the afternoon was the one I feared most, Latin. Archie-Bald, in view of our general stupidity ('Man, you're an ass! Sit down, you donkey!') had let it be known that we must all be present, dead or alive, so that he could cram us for the exams. But before that there were important affairs I had to attend to in the town.

Being cut off at home from the vanman and the postie, it was left to me to do the vital shopping. For this purpose I had been given an old haversack and a long list of necessities to purchase, including a tin of treacle, bread, sausages, tobacco, the mail and newspapers, as well as many other odds and ends. I could see by the length of the list that there would be no hope of visiting the soup kitchen that day, but I could buy a bun or a bar of chocolate on the way. The main thing was to get the messages done.

Unhappily, I was no sooner out of the school gates than a blast of icy wind blew the list out of my hand, and away it sailed over the rector's house, never to be seen again.

For a brief moment I wondered where it would land. In France, or some other foreign country? And what would the natives think of such a strange missive? D-thread, saus., sug., treac., tob., and all the rest.

Then the awfulness of it struck me and I started to shiver with fear rather than cold. All the way up the High Street I tried to visualize the scrawls on the lost list. It was worse than memorizing 'The Brook'.

'Tobacco, sugar, tea, treacle, bread, sausages. I slip, I slide, I gloom, I glance. . . .'

I did what I could, going from shop to shop and swithering on each doorstep. Was it blue darning-thread or brown? Had I to get cookies at the baker's or a pan loaf? What kind of tobacco? How many sausages? Pork or beef? I went to the post office for the letters, to the newsagent for the papers, and finally to the fruit shop for some oranges. I had not had time to buy a bun, but I was past eating.

There were four or five folk in front of me in the shop and I had to stand in line, shuffling my feet and shifting my loaded haversack from one arm to the other. The town clock was nearing the dreaded hour. I prayed for it to slow down and for the folk in front of me to hurry up.

The shopkeeper was a nice enough man, but too good a listener. And the wives who were making their purchases had plenty to tell him, about their varicose veins, the price of apples, and wasn't the weather terrible?

The clock was beginning to chime by the time I took possession of the oranges. 'It must be awful bleak outbye in the storm. Are you not frozen, lass?' he asked, and handed me a banana as a bonus.

'No, I'm fine. Thanks for the banana,' I said hastily, and ran for my life, skidding down the street at top speed. But not quickly enough. The clock had stopped ringing and so had the school bell by the time I came in sight of the gates, only to hear the janitor clashing them shut. When I reached them he was walking away, leaving me gazing through the bars as if I had been shut out of Paradise, though Archie-Bald was hardly my idea of a deity.

I had no notion what to do. Stand and shiver for the rest of the day? Or shout? The janitor had no name, as far as I knew, so all I could call was, 'Janny! Janny!'

He turned round and I could see by that gleam in his eye that I had made his day though I had ruined my own.

'I'm sorry I'm late. Please let me in,' I pleaded.

'No, I'll not,' he said bluntly, and that was that.

For a moment I wondered if I might soften his heart by offering him the banana, but I knew his crust was too hard. He had turned his back on me and was walking away when I gave one last despairing call: 'Janny! Come back! Let me in!'

And then I was aware of someone standing beside me. A large gentleman with a benign look on his face and a clerical collar round his neck. 'Smith! Come back here, Smith!' he called out in a commanding voice.

The janitor turned, gave a start, and came walking back, touching his cap.

'Open the gates, Smith.'

'Yessir!'

It was a miracle, of course; the first nice thing that had happened to me that day. The gleam had gone from the janitor's eye as he turned the key to let me in, and I felt faintly sorry for him. I had spoiled his little hour of triumph.

'Thanks,' I breathed to my saviour – perhaps I should have given *him* the banana – and took to my heels, not stopping to draw breath till I reached the rector's room.

Dafty had not missed me. He was away in one of his dwams, sitting at his desk playing with a paper-clip. The boys gave me a sympathetic glance as I slunk into my seat. I shared the banana with them, a bite each. Unfortunately I was in the midst of chewing mine when Archie-Bald suddenly looked up.

'Stop chewing, girl!' he cried in an irritated growl. (At

least he had called me *girl*.) 'Get on to your feet and read page seven.'

I wondered if the day would ever end, but of course it did. After struggling through algebra ('What does x equal?') the final bell rang at last. The Janny gave me a queer look as I passed out of the gates but I got a warmer welcome from Black Sandy, though he warned me, 'Dod! I doot we'll hae oor troubles on the road oot.' And so we did, for the snow had begun to fall again and it had been dark since early afternoon.

We were in and out of the bus half a dozen times, helping to push it over icy patches, and once we skidded into a snow-filled ditch.

'Heave ho!' roared Black Sandy encouragingly. 'Scots Wha Hae!'

The worst part was my lonely walk in the darkness to reach home. What a relief to see the lights in the windows and to stumble at last into the warm kitchen.

My head was nodding over my supper as I recounted the day to Jessie. But I must have waxed eloquent enough, though I had not noticed her hanging on my words, for at the end she said, 'Mercy, lassie! ye're as guid as the *People's Friend*.'

This was praise indeed. I felt as if Dafty had given me an Excellent Plus mark. It helped to thaw me out as I went to bed clutching my stone hot-water bottle.

There was always the hope that tomorrow might be better.

13. Leisure and Pleasure

Tomorrow was a wonderful word. There was always the prospect of something exciting happening, a new beginning.

It came, and with it the thaw, which meant a return to activity on the farm and an end to listlessness. Strange how the Bible was always right. 'Seedtime and harvest'. Who would have believed, in the depths of winter, that anything could ever grow again on that dead frozen earth? Or that lifeless trees could bring forth fresh shoots? Yet before long the cycle would begin all over again: the ploughing, the sowing, the reaping, the mowing. The hidden flowers would rise like Lazarus from the dead, and the air would be full of bird song.

At the turn of the year the humans, too, began to emerge from their cocoons. All winter long the men had gone about wrapped up 'like dumplings in a cloot' with sometimes only their noses visible. Goodness knows how many layers of woolly sarks and long drawers they wore underneath their corduroys. It was sometimes difficult to tell who was who. 'Are you Wull or Tam?' They both wore khaki-coloured gravats round their necks and sometimes balaclava helmets on their heads.

The herd had a coat with sagging pockets stuffed with miscellaneous objects, medicine for the sheep, his all-purpose knife, a hammer, nails, screws, bolts, binder-twine. He kept his pipe and baccy somewhere in an inner pocket. Often I saw him crouching behind a dyke, as if he was hiding from the enemy, and knew that he was trying to shelter from the blast until he found his pipe and got it going.

During the dark days of winter when the ground lay fallow the men occupied themselves by doing odd jobs about the place, winding straw into ropes, cutting up turnips in an ancient guillotine, chopping sticks, sawing wood, mending implements, crawling about on the roofs to patch up loose slates, and looking after their horses in the work-stable.

Jock-the-herd always had his hands full, especially at lambing time; but the hinds, I felt, grew restless, longing to get back on the land and start ploughing. Sometimes I heard them singing their endless repetitious songs, the cornkisters, so called because farm-workers had a habit of sitting on the cornkist – the wooden corn-chest in the barn – and dunting their feet against its sides in time to their fa-la-las and tooral-oorals.

One of the songs I remember was about an iron horse. What on earth could it be? An iron horse! It was a long time before I solved the mystery and discovered they were singing about a railway train.

'There were hooses in a lang straight line, a' standin' upon
   wheels, man,
And the chiels that fed the horse were as black's a pair o'
   deils, man.
And ne'er a thing they gied the brute, but only coals to eat,
   man.
He was the queerest beast I've seen, for he had wheels for
   feet, man.'

I used to wonder what the men did at night shut up in their small cottages. Sit in their stocking-soles staring into the fire?

They were not the kind to have hobbies, except the herd who spent much of his spare time whittling away at a length of wood, an embryo crook, or polishing its handle. But the hinds just sat. Sometimes they read the local paper, the *Jedburgh Gazette*, or had a look at the *People's Friend* which their wives took in weekly, but there were seldom books to be seen lying about, except the Bible and it was only for the Sabbath.

Now and again they had a game of draughts. In many cottages the dambrod – the draught-board – hung on the wall in pride of place. And I remember Tam saying to Wull, or Wull saying to Tam, after they had finished their tasks in the work-stable, 'I'm thinkin' o' takin' doon the dambrod the nicht. Are ye on for a game?' It was a challenge, like throwing down a glove.

'Richt! I'm on,' said the other, flexing his muscles as if in preparation for a boxing-match.

The game would be like a fiercely fought battle, though little was said by the contestants as they sat opposite each other poring over the board and communicating only by grunts after each move. Next day they replayed it again as they went about their work.

'Ay! I had ye cornered, Tam,' said Wull triumphantly.

'No, ye didny! I could have got oot if I'd tried.'

'Ye could not!'

'I could sot!'

'Weel, what for did ye no' try?'

'I wasny thinkin'. But I'll get ye the next time. . . .' And so it went on.

Sometimes they played dominoes in more light-hearted vein with their wives joining in. But for real jollification a kirn was the thing.

I thought it strange that a kirn, which was the name

Jessie called the churn in which we made butter, should also be the name for a harvest-home, but so it was. A kirn-supper. The first I ever attended was at a large farm in the Oxnam district, and I wonder why I came to be asked to accompany my parents to such a spree? Perhaps it was because there were some young folk in the farmer's family, for I remember dancing an energetic polka with the son of the house, a young gent of nine, destined to become a rugby player. I had bruises on my shins for weeks afterwards, not only from him but from many a tackety boot, for there were no such refinements as dancing-pumps at a good-going kirn.

We drove first to the farmhouse and were piped out to the yard and up the granary stairs where the company was assembled. The rafters had been decorated with greenery and the wooden floor swept well and sprinkled over with soapflakes to make it slippery enough for dancing. It was a strange ballroom, with the cows lowing underneath, the pigs grunting, and a hen appearing from nowhere to peck for loose grain in a corner. But to me it was like fairyland, with the lights from the lanterns swinging overhead softening the scene, the jolly music setting everyone's feet tapping and bringing a sparkle to their eyes. A complete change from anything everyday.

It was the only time I saw Jessie dancing. She was there with her sister Joo-anne and her brother Jock-the-herd. She was still upright, still in a long black skirt, black stockings, black shoes, but wearing a blouse I had never set eyes on before, black, too, but with some shiny ornaments on it and a touch of lace at the neck. What a handsome woman she looked, with her face flushed after executing a Highland Scottische with my father as her partner. He kicked up his heels and hooched with abandon, but Jessie remained dignified, with the same expression on her face as when milking the cows. She had her Sunday stays on for I heard them creaking when I encountered her in the eightsome reel. 'Roond this way, lassie,' she said severely, during the grand chain. 'Ye're gettin' a' fankled.'

I think she was enjoying herself, but she would never let on.

The music was provided by two fiddlers perched precariously on chairs set on top of a small wooden table. They played vigorously in their shirt-sleeves throughout the long dances, stamping their feet to the rhythm and resting now and then when someone was called upon to do a turn.

I was terrified I might be asked to recite, but I need not have worried. There were too many willing volunteers, especially as the night wore on and tongues were loosened after frequent refreshments. The highlight, of course, was my father singing his comic songs. I shouted, 'Encore!' as loud as the rest and laughed at his patter though I knew every word that was coming.

'Isn't he great?' I heard on all sides.

'Oh yes, isn't he?' I agreed. It was not reflected glory. I thought he *was* great.

Others got up and sang sentimental songs ('My Love She's but a Lassie Yet'), the farmer and his wife rendered a duet (The Crookit Bawbee') and the grieve recited an interminable Border ballad, swaying on his feet in the middle of the floor with his eyes firmly closed. Like the brook he went on for ever.

> 'The moon was clear, the day drew near,
> The spears in flinders flew;
> But mony a gallant Englishman
> Ere day the Scotsmen slew.'

The English teacher would have been proud of him, for he never stumbled over a word, but the company began to grow restless and clapped so loudly at the end, with relief, that he took it for an encore.

'I'll gie ye "Tam o' Shanter",' said he, opening his eyes, but luckily we were spared, for just then we were bidden to sit in at the trestle tables set along the sides of the granary, the farmer at the head of one and his wife at the other. It was time for the kirn-supper.

Before we began to eat, the Oxnam minister gave the old Covenanter's grace.

> 'Some hae meat that canna eat,
> And some wad eat that want it;
> But we hae meat, and we can eat,
> And sae the Lord be thankit.'

'A-men!' said the company, and fell to.

It was truly a groaning board, though I cannot recall any detail of the meal, except of drinking a refreshing tumblerful of home-made lemonade and of exchanging conversation-lozenges with my companions.

The young son of the house, flushed with food and long past his bedtime, as, indeed, I was, too, handed me a heart-shaped sweetmeat with 'Do you love me?' printed on it in smudged lettering. The idea! My reply was short and sharp. Fortunately I was in possession of a white lozenge with pink lettering on it. 'Not tonight'. Time and again the sweets changed hands, passing them from one to another, but in the end we ate them all, no matter how grubby they were.

It was strange seeing Jessie sitting still and being served instead of clattering back and forth dishing out potatoes and handing round plates. All the same, she kept a watchful eye on the helpers and I expected her to give them a sharp rebuke when they dropped a fork on the floor or spilt some cream on the tablecloth.

At the end tea was served from a great urn, and the farmer rose to his feet to make a speech of welcome to his friends and thanks to his workers. The unfortunate hind who was to reply had his speech written out on a piece of paper which he held in his trembling hand. He grew purple in the face, petrified with terror when the moment came, and had to be helped on to his feet by his neighbours, with encouraging calls of, 'Come on, Geordie. Do your stuff. Get it aff your chest.'

Somehow or other Geordie stumbled through his stuff and sat down to sympathetic applause, easing his braces and giving a great sigh of relief. It was obvious from the way he gulped at his glass that he was about to enjoy the evening to the full, now that his ordeal was over.

The tables were cleared, the dusty floor re-swept with great stable-brooms and sprinkled once more with soap-flakes. On with the dance. The local minister, a waggish kind of man, came and bowed before me as if I was the Queen of Sheba. 'Would you care to trip the light fantastic with me, young lady?'

I had no idea what he was talking about, but I was flattered, of course, at being called a young lady, and willingly became his partner in the Lancers, during which he whirled me off my feet as if he was an ordinary man and not a servant of God.

The dances were all energetic: Circassian Circle, Roxburgh Castle, Petronella, Triumph, Drops o' Brandy. Some were more like games than dances. It was a sight to see the droopy grieve from Swinside Townhead chasing his wife, the Missis, down the middle and up the sides, ducking and dodging, poussetting and *pas-de-bas*ing. She left a trail of hairpins wherever she went, and it was noticeable that his galluses – like the rest of the company he had long since cast his jacket – were hanging by a thread. But at least he was putting his heart and soul into the dance, which was more than he did with his jobs on the farm.

I felt a glow of pleasure when Jock-the-herd came stramping across the floor to 'lift' me for one of the waltzes the fiddlers played now and again to change the tempo and give the perspiring dancers a breather.

There was no finesse about Jock. 'Man-lassie, come on,' said he, grabbing me by the hand. None of the light fantastic for him. He was heavy on his feet. And mine! Indeed, he danced mainly on his heels, propelling me round and round, to the tune of 'Over the Sea to Skye', as if he was hauling a sack of corn.

'Ane-twa-three, turn! Ane-twa-three, turn!'

Sometimes he tried to reverse, with disastrous results. The other dancers jostled and bumped us back into place till I felt like a football. Still, it was a treat to be dancing with Jock and I would not have changed partners for Rudolph Valentino if he had suddenly appeared in the granary and knelt at my feet to beg for a waltz.

The cocks were crowing and the grey light of dawn creeping into the granary by the time the fiddlers played the last dance, a roundabout waltz called the Hoolachan in which everyone joined, changing partners as they progressed round the floor. Then we all clasped hands to sing 'Auld Lang Syne', gave three cheers for the farmer, and made our ways home, some not too steadily.

The story is told of a farmworker who had been imbibing too freely at a kirn and was making such a nuisance of himself that he was repeatedly asked to leave. In the end he had to be forcibly removed, at which point he was heard to mutter, 'A'weel, I dinna care. It's been a gey dry affair, onywey.'

Strange how everyone seemed to be crosser after an evening's jollity. Next day Jessie had an attack of her mysterious ailment called the bile, and kept her lips in a thin tight line. I knew better than to talk to her. Now and then she took sips of hot water and thumped her stomach angrily before giving a belch. Even Jock was a bit grumpy, and when I asked him how he had enjoyed the kirn mumbled something about a 'sair heid'. Even I felt dizzy through lack of sleep. It seemed one had to pay dearly for one's pleasures, but oh! they were worth it.

It was better than a tonic from the doctor to explode now and again and let feelings go free instead of always bottling them up. Borderers have a habit of fencing themselves in, encasing their minds in armour as restricting as Jessie's stays, so that no one can ever guess their innermost thoughts.

The most they will ever say to each other in meeting is, 'Nice day.'

'Ay, no' bad.'

Or, like Jessie and Jock when they met in the farmyard, pass each other with scarcely a grudging grunt of recognition.

'What do you talk about at night, Jessie?' I once asked her. 'You and Jock and Joo-anne?'

'Naethin'.'

Maybe the feeling was there, deep down. The pity was it never came to the surface.

This reticence, I felt, ruined many a relationship. Even as a bairn, I sensed it myself. There were times when I longed to run after Jessie, throw my arms round her neck, and say, 'Oh, Jessie! I love you!' But I could never bring myself to do it. What would be her reaction? 'Away, lassie! Dinna be daft.'

Or, might it have been that she, like the rest of us, was waiting for a sign of affection? And all of us afraid to take the first step.

But it would have taken a bold soul to bell a Border cat!

14 Spring-Cleaning

After the turn of the year the hinds were eager to get on with the ploughing. It seemed to give them some inward satisfaction to see the long straight furrows in the fields and to know that the familiar cycle had started once more. For weeks beforehand they had been examining the ploughs in the cart-shed, seeing that the cutting-blades were in good order, and mentally flexing their muscles for the work ahead.

Now that I was going to town each day I had gained some small degree of importance in their eyes, for not only could I do little bits of shopping for them, I was also learning to keep my eyes open so that I could pass on useful information.

'They've started ploughing at Sunlaws.' Or the Bairnkine, or one of the other farms I passed in the school bus.

'Weel then, we'll need to get on. Tell the Boss.'

But they knew, and so did the Boss, that Overton Bush was outbye and the other farms inbye. They were more sheltered, with softer soil. Why risk breaking the ploughshares on ground that was still as hard as iron? The day would come when a warmer spell of weather would make the earth yield, then out would come the Clydesdales with their great stamping feet and tossing heads. Operation ploughing would begin.

When the first bright rays of spring sunshine penetrated through the farmhouse windows, showing up all the deficiencies hidden during the dark days of winter: the dusty corners, the damp patches on the ceilings, the faded cushions, the torn wallpaper, another operation far deadlier than the ploughing was under way. The spring-cleaning. Everything in the house was upside-down – 'tapsulteerie', Jessie said – and for weeks we lived in such discomfort that Father shut himself up in the greenhouse and I escaped to the ruined castle as often as I could.

I often wondered why anyone bothered, for no one seemed to enjoy it. But it was the done thing. Perhaps nobody would have started at all if it had not been for inquisitive enquiries from neighbouring farmers' wives. 'Have you started the cleaning yet? Oh yes, we're well on. Papered the spare room yesterday. Pink roses. You should have seen the *oose* below the bed!' (*Oose* was the dusty fluff that collected below beds and in unswept corners.) 'How far on are you? Not started yet! Oh well!'

We were made to feel outcastes.

It was not just a cursory cleaning. Every single piece of furniture had to be moved from its moorings, every item of bedding, every curtain and carpet was taken outside to be given an airing. And a beating. I can still see Mother and Jessie standing one at each side of a carpet slung over the clothes-rope in the back garden, belabouring it in turn with stout sticks till their arms ached, while clouds of dust rose up into the air after every blow.

It all had to be done the hard way. What would they have made of today's labour-saving aids to instant cleaning:

electric polishers, spin-dryers, dish-washers and all the rest? Elbow-grease was their greatest asset. And Jessie and the servant-girl used plenty of that in the course of their every-day tasks, with waxcloth to be polished, grates blackleaded, fire-irons rubbed with emery paper, tables scrubbed, cutlery cleaned with bath-brick, doorsteps washed and milk-pails scoured. Little wonder their arms were so sinewy and their hands so rough.

It was not just elbow-grease that was needed at the spring-cleaning. Staying-power was the thing. Relentlessly they went on day after day, turning out one room after another, even the garret which looked strangely tidy the next time I was sent to solitary confinement, but it did not take me long to get it back into its higgledy-piggledy mess.

One of my own tasks was to take all the books out of the bookcases, bang them about to get rid of the 'stoor' and dust them down before replacing them in neat rows on the shelves. It was impossible during this process not to dip into *Black Beauty* or *Lamb's Tales*, or to have a keek inside an old primer belonging to a past generation. At the bottom of each page there was an uplifting saying. One I remember was, 'Go to the ant, thou sluggard, consider her ways, and be wise.'

It was good advice but I did not benefit from it until Jessie found me sitting on the floor surrounded by piles of undusted books and gave me a sharp reminder to look slippy.

The worst part of the cleaning, to my mind, was the tossing, turning and airing of all the mattresses from the beds. Each had to be dragged outside, beaten to death, and left propped over garden seats till it was time to haul them back into the house again. Jessie called them the *tykabeds*.

A tykabed was one of the first household necessities a young woman acquired for her 'doon-sittin'' when she was about to settle in to her new home on her marriage and which saw her through her lifetime. Some folk, according to Jessie, became so attached to their own tykabeds (in a manner of speaking) that nothing would induce them to sleep on any other.

'But what did they do if they went on their holidays?' I once asked her.

'Sent their tykabeds on in a cairt,' she declared.

I wondered what would have happened to our own mattresses if we had sent them in advance to the seaside along with the tin trunk. Indeed, at the spring-cleaning, I often wished we could send them away never to return, especially the feather-beds.

I had a kind of love-hate for the fluffy mattresses on which some of us slept. It was bliss on a cold night to sink into such a soft nest, but there was always the terror that it would engulf me while I was asleep, and often I woke up, fighting my way out for fear of being smothered. I preferred a harder resting-place, but it was all the luck of the draw. The beds and the sleepers thereon were chopped and changed depending on the exigencies of the moment.

At the cleaning the covers had to be washed, and the contents taken out to be picked over and sorted through. A fresh supply of clean feathers had been collected during the year and kept in a large white bolster-case to be added to the reconditioned feather-bed. This was a tricky performance not to be undertaken on a windy day when the feathers would fly through the air like snowflakes. I sometimes saw the hens pecking at them, blissfully unaware that they, too, would be plucked in due course.

Now and again Father emerged from the greenhouse and wandered about like a lost soul. There was no comfortable place for him to settle in the house, with carpets rolled up, chairs piled on top of tables, brooms and buckets everywhere, and nothing in its rightful place. Sometimes he was forced to lend a hand by knocking in a nail here and there, putting up a curtain-rail or whitewashing a ceiling. But he was not really a handyman. I was sure that one of the comic songs he sang had been specially written for him.

'When Father papered the parlour
You couldn't see him for paste.
Dabbing it here, dabbing it there,
Paste and paper everywhere.
Mother got stuck to the ceiling,
The kids were stuck to the floor,
You never saw a bloomin' family
So stuck up before.'

Once in a while we were forced to send for a real trades-
man to do a professional job. These were big occasions in
our lives, for the plumber or paper-hanger had to come all
the way out from Jedburgh and stay for the entire day,
sometimes even overnight, till the job was finished. I found
it fascinating to watch how they set about their work with
such skill, and admired the ease with which they used blow-
lamps, took doors off their hinges, unscrewed plugs, tore up
floor-boards, or scraped paper off the walls. It seemed a
miracle that they could ever put things back to rights again,
but somehow they did.

Jessie was for ever telling them not to make a *slaister*, a
slaister being a mess. She was in no way intimidated by
workmen, no matter how professional, and soundly rated
one who left his dirty finger-marks on a clean wall. 'I've a
guid mind to gie ye a skelpin'.' But she always had the
kettle boiling and a meal of sorts ready for them when she
felt they had earned a 'sit doon' at the kitchen table.

The new wallpaper had been chosen weeks in advance,
with my mother going through a sample book page by page,
pondering over flowery patterns for the spare bedroom or
whirly designs for the dining-room, the busier the better.
Nothing plain. Lying in bed in the candlelight I fancied I
could see 'things' on the walls, witches and warlocks hiding
behind sprays of violets, or huntsmen chasing their prey
through clumps of cornflowers.

It was a pity we never had the sewing-woman to stay. I
had heard tales of Shewin' Sarah who went around the

countryside with her portmanteau, staying for days at a time at various homesteads where she made curtains, mended breeks, repaired sheets and passed on tittle-tattle from one household to another. Mother and Jessie had already done the making and mending and had no need of extra help, but I would have liked to listen to Sarah's gossip and maybe get a new frock made from a different pattern.

I used to feel sorry for the 'body' when she was brought down from the garret to be used as a model. She got so many pins and needles stuck into her. But Jessie used to scoff at me and say, 'Hoots-toots! she's only a dummy. She canna feel a thing. Pass me the pirrn.'

The reels of cotton were the pirrns, the pins were the preens, and the stitches the steeks. Jessie's steeks were sewn so firmly that they were there for life, and no button ever left its mooring once she had stitched it firmly into place.

My job if I was there was to thread the needle, for though Jessie would never admit her eyes were not as sharp as mine, her own attempts often ended in failure. It was the needles that were at fault, she declared. They were making the eyes too small these days.

Many of my garments were hand-me-doons or concocted out of discarded curtains. Jessie had only one pattern, take it or leave it. No frills, fancies or finery.

'Could I not have a wee bit lace for a change?' I would sometimes plead.

'Lace!' said she, with her mouth full of preens. 'Set ye up! What are ye wantin' lace for, an' you aye climbin' trees?'

I liked the whirring sound the wheezy old sewing-machine made as the needle leapt from one stitch to another, but though Jessie pedalled away with a will she preferred sewing by hand. 'The steeks last langer.'

There was no sitting down and sewing during the spring-cleaning. We were all up and at it, stopping only for scratch meals when anyone had time to cook them. Indeed, on the day the kitchen chimney was swept we were lucky if we got a hot meal at all. Father and one of the hinds did the deed, ending up as black as darkies, with sacks of soot to be dragged outside and trails left on the kitchen floor. If ever Jessie used the word slaister it was then!

Throughout the year she sometimes set the lum alight herself, to clear away the cumulation, taking pages of the *Scotsman*, putting a match to them and thrusting them as far as she could up the chimney. I always ran out to see the sparks flying sky high and to hear the roar of the flames if the chimney really went on fire.

'It's on haud!' Jessie would cry, grabbing the shovel to catch the avalanche of red-hot soot that came tumbling down into the fireplace. All the pots and pans had been cleared out of the way and Blackie, the kitchen cat, had taken refuge under the table.

Afterwards the sticks and coals burned more brightly in the grate and the servant-lassie had less trouble lighting the fire in the morning. Liz-Ann, the Cairthorse, always had difficulty in coaxing the kindling into life. She would go down on her hunkers and try to fan the flames by blowing into the fireplace until she was red in the face. Or she would seize the bellows and blast away with all her might. Sometimes in desperation she sprinkled paraffin on the sticks, risking scorched eyebrows and worse, a ticking-off from Jessie.

Taking up the stair-carpet, beating the dust out of it, polishing the rods, and laying it back again step by step with its underfelt in place, was one of the most tedious tasks at the cleaning. Each stair had to be washed and scrubbed, and strict warnings were given that we were not to traipse up and down in dirty shoes. There seemed no place to turn for comfort. Tempers grew shorter as the house became cleaner, till everyone was squabbling. 'Catter-batterin',' Jessie called it.

It was a wonderful day when I heard her say, 'That's it

feenished,' and the last ornament was put back into place. For a time it was difficult to settle in such a spotless house. The homeliness seemed to have rubbed off with the elbow-grease. Father grumbled that he 'couldn't find a thing', but Mother was pleased with the results, worn out though she was with her efforts. I sometimes watched her standing back to admire her handiwork, with a look of satisfaction on her face. Then, trying to look guileless she would say, 'I think I'll just ring up the Scotts.'

I would hear her at the telephone saying smugly, 'The spring-cleaning? Oh yes, we're through! New curtains in the spare bedroom and we've re-papered the dining-room. You must come for your tea soon.'

It was all over for another year. But, like our sins white-washed every Sunday, the purity would not last long. We were soon back to our old topsy-turvy ways, oose below the beds, cluttered cupboards, untidy drawers, and muddles on every chair and sofa. To tell the truth, I liked it better that way.

Every year nature did its own spring-cleaning with far less fuss, as if an unseen hand had been busy with spit and polish. The primroses suddenly appeared by the burnside, the buds opened out on the trees, and there was a clean sparkle in the sky as if it, too, had been scrubbed with soapy water. The sun was still feeble and the weather a mixture of smiles and tears, but warm enough to coax the seeds to sprout and the wild flowers in the meadow to show their faces.

It was a young hopeful time, the silly season for lambs, chicks, foals and calves. Humans, too, who walked with sprightlier steps and gave way to sudden bursts of whistling. With the rising of the sap, I too, felt an urge to do something special, to fight for my country or save the Chinese from famine. (Jessie was always telling me how the starving Chinese would be glad of my discarded crusts.) But I had to content myself with helping the herd when he was mending a drystone dyke. Not that he appreciated my assistance.

'Man-lassie, get oot ma road an' I'll get on quicker.'

My attempts at beautifying the doorstep with pipe-clay were no better received. I tried to liven the look of it by putting my art lessons into practice. A flower here, a vase there, an apple, an orange (still life) all joined together with curly loops till there was not a vacant space left. It was an impressive sight, I thought, but not to Jessie.

'Wumman, hae ye nae gumption!' she raged. 'Ye'll gliff folk awa'. An' did ye no' think o' *weshin'* the doorstep first?'

The road to hell, the minister told us, is paved with good intentions. But the day came when I got the chance to prove my worth.

15. Another Blue Day

That day I had taken particular notice of the text on the wall. It was written by someone called T. Carlyle.

So here hath been dawning
Another blue Day;
Think, wilt thou let it
Slip useless away?

It was Saturday and I was free for the whole day. And there was blue in the sky. So what could I do to fill the fleeting hours with something worthwhile? I might do my homework and learn some of Dafty's Latin or Miss Crichton's French, but how would that help the starving Chinese?

'Would you like to do a good deed?' Mother asked me at breakfast, as if reading my thoughts. 'You could go round collecting.'

'Collecting what?'

'Money, of course.' She handed me a tattered notebook. 'For the Schemes of the Church.'

I had no notion what the church was scheming, but it would likely be something good, so here was my opportunity. I hastily finished my porridge and had a look inside the notebook. It was filled with smudged names and addresses of all the folk in the district who had contributed their shillings and sixpences last year. My task would be to call on each one and extract the same amount this year. Or more, if I was lucky; in which case T. Carlyle would surely be pleased with my efforts.

The only way to go my rounds was by Shanks's pony. The old boneshaker bicycle was in no fit state to carry me far, and many of my ports of call could only be reached by trudging across the braes; but who wanted to achieve martyrdom the easy way? The harder the road the higher marks I would gain from up above.

I set off like a pilgrim carrying an old handbag of my mother's in which to collect the money. There were a few false starts before I could shake off various followers who wanted to accompany me, including the banty hen, the pet lamb, and a small child who had toddled up from the cottages, hoping I would play with her.

'Hide-and-theek?' she lisped.

'No, not today. I've got things to do,' I said importantly.

'Can I no' do thingth, too?'

'No, you can't. Go away home.'

Her bottom lip began to tremble, and I hunted in Mother's handbag in the hope of finding a sweetie there, a leftover pandrop from the church, but there was only a hairpin and a stub of a pencil.

'Here, have the pencil,' I said, thrusting it at wee Maggie. It was better than nothing.

'Oh, thankth,' she said, beginning to suck it there and then. 'Will you play hide-and-theek when you come back?'

'Maybe,' I said cautiously, and hurried away on my mission.

It was flattering to feel wanted if only by wee Maggie,

but I had bigger things to do than hide behind haystacks.

My first encounter with danger came when the bull snorted after me as I was traversing the hill on my way across to a neighbouring farm called Stotfield. He pawed the ground and came close enough for me to hang Mother's handbag on his horns if I had been daft enough, but I had sufficient sense to sidle towards the dyke and scramble over like lightning, doing my stockings no good in the process. Perhaps the beast was only being friendly, but I was learning a modicum of gumption and it was better not to take risks at the start of my pilgrimage.

I had to approach my objective by a roundabout route through a dark wood filled with eerie rustlings, where beasties and bogles seemed to lurk behind every tree. It was only the thought of the halo on my head that kept me going. Onward Christian soldier.

It was a relief to emerge at the other side and see a friendly house in the distance. The dogs came out to meet me, barking and frisking. There were familiar cacklings and grunts from the farmyard, and the wife herself came to the door, welcoming the sight of any stranger, even me.

'Come in. The kettle's on the boil. What's the news?'

I tried to tell her about the Schemes of the Church, but what she wanted was local gossip, the schemes of Overton Bush, Camptown and Edgerston. While she toasted bread on a long pronged fork in front of the fire she plied me with questions. How had we got on with the spring-cleaning? Had I heard that Mary-Anne's varicose veins had broken out? Was it true that the minister's wife had been left a fortune? Fifty pounds from her auntie in Edinburgh. She was going to buy a new fur coat with it, so it was said, and a carpet for the minister's study. High time, too. Had I noticed how threadbare the old one was?

For one who lived so far off the beaten track Mrs Stotfield seemed surprisingly up to date with the news. I wondered if Shewin' Sarah had visited her lately.

She handed me a slice of pan-loaf, evenly toasted on each side, and pushed a jar of bramble jelly within reach. Then she delivered a bombshell.

'I hear your mother's expecting again.'

'What?'

I was so stunned, the very thought put me off my toast.

For a moment I wondered if Mother herself knew, then realized that, of course, she must. Living on a farm I had learned enough of the facts of life to know that babies were not found under gooseberry bushes. The news was both exciting and depressing. If Mrs Stotfield's story was true it meant I would be pushed further out of the nest and become even more of a nonentity. Yet it would bring a bit of stir about the place, with the doctor coming and going, the monthly nurse in residence and the prospect of another christening in the parlour.

Having drained me dry of news and at the same time given me plenty to think about Mrs Stotfield now began to rummage in the dresser drawer for her purse but could only raise ninepence in assorted coins, which was threepence less than last time. So I felt a poor missionary for the church as I left the house with her calling after me, 'Mind an' tell your mother I was asking for her. Maybe it'll be twins this time.'

I did better with the gamekeeper whom I met striding across the braes with a gun below his oxter, and saved myself a long trail to call at his cottage door. I always felt that the Gamey, with his white beard and wise sayings, looked like Moses in the Bible, and would not have been surprised if he kept the ten commandments in his game bag, but it was usually a live ferret or a dead pheasant.

When I told him my mission he thrust his hand in his pocket and brought out a silver shilling.

'You're only down for sixpence,' I told him truthfully, taking a look in the notebook. 'D'you want change?'

'No, the kirk could be doing with it.' He gazed up at the

sky as if it was the Promised Land. 'The ways of the Lord are wonderful to behold. Think of all the folk up there in heaven, and millions more maybe on the planets.'

But I was thinking of something more practical. 'Could you lend me a pencil, please?' I had to write his name in the notebook, and Mrs Stotfield's, too, and was regretting my generous gesture to wee Maggie. The Schemes of the Church would get all mixed up if I had to do mental arithmetic and keep a note of everybody's contributions in my head.

The Gamey hunted in his pockets and brought forth an assortment of string, wire, nails, knives and matchboxes. No pencil. 'Ah well, the Lord will provide,' he said, hoisting up his gun and going on his way.

The Lord provided at my next port of call, the cluster of cottages near the Big Hoose where the estate workers for the laird lived. It was easy going from one to the other instead of trudging miles across the hills .The gardener gave me a pencil and sharpened it into such a fine point that it broke as soon as I started to write Mrs Stotfield's name.

'Ye're pressin' ower hard, wumman,' said he, and sharpened it again. I was more careful next time and succeeded in keeping my accounts in order, even spelling the names correctly. But it was a worrying job and I felt I was not really cut out for big business.

One of my most terrifying tasks was to call at the Big Hoose. I was petrified in case I might meet the laird himself and prayed that he would be away in London. It was a deed that had to be done, for he was the biggest contributor in the book. Ten shillings. If I missed him, my takings would plummet to the depths.

I went round to the back door hoping to hand in the book to his housekeeper and perhaps get threepence from her, too, but who should advance towards me from the kitchen garden but Himself, wearing shabby old knickerbockers and carrying a spade in his hand? Fancy the laird digging! We were face to face so there was no chance of my darting away.

'Hullo,' he said, eyeing me from his great height. 'What are you doing here?'

'C-Collecting for the Schemes of the Ch-Church.'

'Oh!' I could see he had no idea what *they* were, but catching sight of the notebook in my hand he asked, 'What did I give last time?'

'Ten shillings.'

It seemed a fortune, even for such a wealthy man, but the laird did not blench. Instead, he took out a pocket book, extracted a pound note and handed it to me. 'There! Will that do?'

I was flabbergasted at receiving such a vast sum of money and carefully tucked it away in Mother's handbag beside the humbler coins. The man must be a millionaire, though at this moment with mud on his boots and his shirt-sleeves rolled up he looked almost like an ordinary human being.

He made some other remark, but in such a high-falutin' voice that I could not translate it, then held out his hand. For a moment I thought he wanted his pound back but he was only saying goodbye. It was strange shaking hands with God. Mine were grubby enough but so were his, so I parted from him feeling more or less on even terms.

I came down with a bump while traversing a wild stretch of moorland at the foothills of the Cheviots to reach my farthest away shepherd's cottage. There was no road to it, only a beaten track. Agnes, the herd's daughter, was a middle-aged severe-looking woman, seldom seen except once a week at the church. She had never been known to converse with anyone. 'Uh-huh!' was as much as she would say.

'She keeps hersel' to hersel',' Jessie used to declare; but maybe I could break through the barriers. Clever me.

I was thinking out a line of approach – perhaps it would interest her to hear that my mother was expecting – when a dreaded roar startled me. 'Hull – oo – a!' It was Yorkie, the gentleman tramp who roamed the country on both sides of the Borders and who often turned up at our farm demanding food and shelter. He was said to be a harmless lunatic, but we were all afraid of him, for there was no knowing when he might turn ugly. It all depended on the moon, according to Yorkie himself. Even in daylight I kept well out of his way, but there was no escape here on the bleak moorland with not a bush or a tree to hide behind.

He came lurching towards me with a crazed look in his eyes, brandishing his stick and talking gibberish to himself. I hastily hid the handbag behind my back, feeling I must defend the church's funds to the death. What if Yorkie got hold of the laird's pound note?

I need not have worried for he brushed past me as if I did not exist and continued to 'Hull-oo-a!' as he went on his way. It was a relief to see him stumbling into the distance, but the encounter had left me shaken, and my candle was not burning quite so brightly by the time I reached the cottage door.

It was open and all was still inside. I could hear the ticking of the wag-at-the-wa' – the clock on the wall – and the clicking of knitting-needles. Agnes was sitting at the kitchen table turning the heel of a sock. In front of her was a batch of newly baked barley scones propped up on their sides to cool. All the baking-dishes had been tidied away and everything was spotless, not a speck of dust, not a thing out of place, as if she did a perpetual spring-cleaning every day. Agnes herself was all-in-the-one-piece, as Jessie would say. Black skirt, black blouse, black apron, black hair tightly drawn back into a bun; and a black frown on her brow.

She did not look up when I gave a tentative knock at the open door and said, 'Hullo.' Unlike all the other houses I had visited there was no warm welcome here. No cry of, 'Come in. What's the news?' Agnes ignored my presence. She was knitting a sock, and that was that.

'I've come to collect for the Schemes of the Church.

You're down for ninepence.' I was not going away without it, after trudging so far across the moor.

'Uh-huh!' she acknowledged, and continued knitting till she reached the end of the row. Was her life so regulated and self-contained that she had no need of outside diversions, no desire to communicate with other human beings? Perhaps she had forgotten how to laugh and speak.

I wondered if her everyday tasks gave her all the satisfaction she needed. Cleaning the house, milking the cow, feeding the hens, making butter, washing, turning the heel of a sock. What did she say to her father, the shepherd, when he came in from the hills after his day's work? 'Uh-huh!' and set his food in front of him?

Presently she got up, went to the dresser drawer and carefully counted out ninepence from an old leather purse with a strong clasp on it. I thought I would break the silence by saying something, so I told her that Yorkie had just gone past. She took no notice. Yorkie had gone past, so what else was there to say? She handed me the money and went back to her knitting. My visit was over.

'Ta-ta,' I said half-heartedly, and went away musing on the mysteries of the world and the strangeness of other folk's lives. The laird in his Big Hoose, Mary-Anne talking to her hens, Yorkie with his head full of mad notions, Dafty at the Grammar School bursting into sudden rages, the Gamey seeing things in the sky, Black Sandy shouting, 'Gee-up!' to the school bus. All made from the same mould and yet so different.

Who was I? What was my role in life? A runner and fetcher! 'Run and fetch the Boss.' 'Run upstairs and fetch down the bedroom lamps.' 'Run and chase the pig out of the garden.'

I was suddenly mindful of an old man at the farm, the father of one of the hinds, who drank himself to death, with water. His thirst was so fierce that he could literally have drunk the burn dry.

I remember the first time he shouted to me, when he was out helping in the fields, 'Rin, lassie, an' fetch me some waitter.'

'In a tumbler?' I asked.

'No, no. A pail.'

I can see him clasping the pail with both hands and feverishly drinking from it, like a horse at the trough. But it never seemed to slake his thirst.

'Rin back an' fill it again,' he would say when he had drained the last drop. 'Ay, lassie, ye're a great rinner an' fetcher.'

It was the first funeral I had ever seen, when the old man died. From a distance I watched the sad procession of men, dressed like black crows, carrying the mysterious box out of one of the cottages and bearing it away. The man's thirst was cured at last.

Running and fetching, I supposed was better than just standing still. And it bore results. By the time I had finished my rounds and reached Granny's cottage at Camptown I was a wealthy woman. The heaviness of my handbag was proof that I had not let another blue day slip useless away. Granny gave me threepence, which was all she could afford, poor body, and let me have a dip into the sweetie-box on the mantelpiece. I did a bit of running and fetching for her, too, carrying in sticks from 'round the back', filling her kettle, and dusting the top of the wardrobe which she could never reach.

As I neared Bella Confectionery's shop the devil crept up behind me and whispered in my ear. 'Think what you could buy with all that money. Jujubes, caramels, pandrops, liquorice-allsorts. Mountains of home-made toffee. It would be easy enough to fiddle the books. The laird's contribution, for instance. You could pretend he only gave you ten shillings, the same as last year, then you would have the rest to spend. Ten shillings' worth of chocolate-drops, all to yourself!'

I could taste them in my mouth, sweet and cloying, hundreds and thousands of them.

I walked past the shop, of course, but I still felt a sinner at heart for the wicked thought had been there. The last climb up the steep farm road was the worst. My legs were aching by now and I was not as pleased with myself as I had been. But it was nice to smell kippers frying when I finally reached the farmhouse and to see my mother laying out the knives and forks on the table. I took a quick glance at her but I could not tell whether she was expecting or not. She just seemed the same.

'You're back,' she said without turning round. 'Good! You can run and shut in the hens before you have your supper.'

It was not easy being a pilgrim.

16. Uncertainties

There always seemed to be a touch of magic in the air when the first call of the cuckoo was heard near the farmhouse. There was something alluring about the sound, but try as I would I never succeeded in seeing the elusive bird. He was only a wandering voice.

'Where is't?' I would puzzle, running through the wood to the cow-gang trying in vain to locate the mocking sound, at once far off and near. It was like playing a game of hide-and-seek with an invisible companion.

> The cuckoo is a bonny bird,
> He sings as he flies;
> He brings us good tidings;
> He tells us no lies.
>
> He drinks the cold water
> To keep his voice clear,
> And he'll come again
> In the spring of the year.

Jessie called him the gowk. (She called me a gowk, too, but that was a different matter.) And she sometimes talked about a gowk-storm, which was a sudden tempestuous squall in the early part of the year. Where did she cull all her knowledge? From bound volumes of the *Quiver*, from the sheep-dip calendar, or the *People's Friend*? Maybe she had been born with it in her head. I felt she could have taught Auld Baldy-Heid a thing or two. And Dafty at the Grammar School as well.

But she knew nothing about French.

I was sitting idly swaying on the swing, listening to the cuckoo calling and doing my home-lessons in my head, in a sort of a way.

> '*Allons, enfants de la patrie,*
> *Le jour de gloire est arrivé. . . .*'

Miss Crichton had been trying to teach us the Marseillaise, which was like Scots Wha Hae to the Frenchies, but that was as far as I could go. What came next?

'Cuck – oo – oo – oo!'

Jessie emerged from the kitchen door with a little three-cornered shawl thrown over her shoulders, on her way home to the herd's hoose, her day's work done. I was about to shout, 'What's next, Jessie?' when I realized it was no use asking her. She thought little enough of English let alone French. Anything other than broad Border Scots was a heathen tongue.

I watched her as she walked away. There was something about Jessie's back view that brought a pang of pain to my heart. Could it be a foreboding that she was going away for ever?

All the sad thoughts of youth came tumbling into my head. The uncertainties about the future, above all the dread of death.

But Jessie was invulnerable. Wasn't she?

'Cuck – oo – oo – oo!'

The bird seemed to be jeering at me. Surely, surely nothing could happen to Jessie.

As if sensing my fear she turned round and gave me one of her direct looks.

'I'll see ye the morn's mornin', lassie.'

My heart leapt up. 'Right, Jessie,' I cried and swung myself sky high. Never mind the Marseillaise. I began to sing one of Black Sandy's songs instead.

> 'Come, love, come, the boat lies low,
> She lies high and dry on the O-hi-o! . . .'

If I flew high enough and looked in the right direction I could catch a glimpse of the Eildon hills away in the distance. Like Jessie they never changed. And if I twirled round the other way I fancied I could see the top of Big Cheviot, equally steadfast.

I watched the hinds going down the road walking side by side in their big tackety boots, on their way home to supper. Then the herd came by carrying a lump of wood in his arms.

'What's that, Jock?'

'Wud.'

'What for?'

'Naethin'. It'll come in handy. Man-lassie, look oot or ye'll tummle.'

'No, I'll not. Swing me higher, Jock, please.'

'Nae fears. I'll awa' an' split the wud. It'll mak' guid kinlin' for the fire.'

There was something about his back view, too, as he walked away that brought back that vague feeling of uncertainty.

'Jock!' I called out urgently.

'Eh?'

'Nothing's going to change, is it?'

He half turned and stood for a moment not scoffing at me but pondering over the question.

'A'weel, the Borders'll aye be here, onwey.'

It was almost a reassurance. Enough, anyway, to dispel my fears.

> 'Come, love, come, won't you come along with me?
> I'll take you down to Ten-nes-see.'

Next morning the worst of my forebodings were realized, though by that time I had forgotten all about them and came skipping into the kitchen as bright as a bee. Another Saturday morning with a whole blue day to myself.

'Jessie! I'm ready for my breakfast.'

She was not there.

Her sister Joo-anne, in a clean white pinny, was stirring the porridge.

I stared at her blankly. 'Where's Jessie?'

'She's d-d-d . . .' Joo-anne always spoke with a slight stammer, especially when she was excited. At first I thought she was trying to tell me Jessie was dead. 'She's d-doon.'

'Doon?'

'Wi' her st-st-stamoch.'

'Mercy me!' I stood there looking at Joo-anne and still not taking it in. 'Is she – is she awful ill?'

'Daursay no. She'll be f-fine. Get oot me r-r-road, lassie. Sit doon an' eat your br-br-breakfast.'

She was nice, was Joo-anne, but she was not Jessie. How could I swallow my porridge or do justice to the succulent ham that was frizzling in the frying-pan? I could only think of Jessie being 'doon'. All I wanted was to go to the herd's hoose and see for myself.

Never before had she given in to any illness. The rest of us came out in spots, took 'hoasts' or whooping-cough, broke our ankles, cracked our noses, or caught ringworm. Not Jessie. Illness was something to be ignored. 'Stop thinkin' aboot it an' it'll gang awa',' was her creed.

I ran all the way through the fields. If the cuckoo was calling I did not hear him. I wanted to take Jessie a present, but what? A minding of some kind. I could stop and pick a bunch of wild flowers but they would be wilted by the time I reached her cottage. Suddenly I saw something glinting on the grass, the sheen of a feather, made up of a mixture of greens and blues and deep reds, with a clean white quill at the end. Maybe Jessie would like it. I stooped to pick it up and ran on.

The door was on the latch. I lifted the sneck and walked in. Jessie was in the box bed, not lying down but sitting bolt upright in a white nightdress – her goonie – with her hair in a spirally pigtail, thumping angrily at her chest as if trying to hit the pain away.

'Oh, Jessie!' I could not think of anything else to say.

She gave me a sharp look and said crossly, 'What's up? What are ye here for?'

'I – I came to see you, Jessie.'

'A'weel, ye've seen me.' She turned her head to the wall as if to hide the pain and the fact that she had been caught off guard.

'Is it the bile, Jessie?' I knew, though she always tried to hide it, that Jessie suffered from a recurring ailment which had something to do with heartburn and wind in the stomach. 'Can I not do anything?'

She screwed up her face. 'Pit the kettle on.'

I knew what she meant, for I had seen her often enough in the kitchen at home, sipping piping-hot water which seemed to relieve the pain. So I laid down the feather on her bed, swung the kettle on the swey and waited till the water was hot enough. Then I filled a cup and handed it to her. For a time she sipped and thumped, thumped and sipped, while I waited for the explosion.

At last it came. She let out a loud long satisfying 'rift'.

'*That*'s better!' I said, as pleased as punch. 'How are you feeling now, Jessie?'

'Hoots, I'm fine.' There was more colour in her cheeks and she had stopped thumping her chest, but she was still angry at having been caught with her defences down. 'Awa' hame,' she ordered me. 'Awa' an' gie Joo-anne a hand.'

But as I made my way to the door she seemed to relent a little and said in a softer voice, 'If ye look in the dresser drawer ye'll mebbe find a sweetie.'

I went home sucking the treacle toffee, not sure whether to feel happy or sad. Jessie was not dying, but she had shaken my belief in the permanence of life. The farmhouse in front of me looked strong and solid, but would it crumble to ashes one day? How much time was left?

'Cuck – oo – oo – oo!'

The mocking bird had come back but he had no answer to give.

I was eager to go to church next day. The Sabbath. Not to hear the minister quoting, 'Verily, I say unto you,' or to listen to his long driech discourse. I wanted to have a private word with God. 'Make Jessie well. Let everything stay the same as it is. For ever and ever, Amen.'

I waited till all the folk were in, the laird and his lot rustling their way up to the gallery. Was that strange little man with him Sir J. M. Barrie? He looked like a gnome, perching in his pew and peering down at the commoners in the body of the kirk.

Everyone looked different on Sundays in their good clothes and with solemn expressions on their faces. Had they dressed up for God, I wondered, or for their fellow-worshippers? Even Big Bob's hair and been slicked down and Mrs Stotfield's costume showed signs of having been pressed with a hot iron.

I looked across at the picture of the Good Shepherd on the stained-glass window, and just then our own shepherd came in, doffing his bowler hat. This was the moment I always waited for, to see the steam rising from Jock-the-herd's bald head. Joo-anne followed him, carefully turning up the back of her costume jacket before settling in the pew.

Then – goodness gracious! – who was that upright figure

marching in to join them? Jessie herself! A shade paler than usual, her lips a little tighter, but how wonderful it was to see her. Everything was back to normal.

I wanted to call across to her, 'Jessie! It's great to see you.' But we were on our feet singing the opening paraphrase, with Miss Todd, the organist, pedalling away at full steam.

> 'Let not your hearts with anxious thoughts
> Be troubled or dismayed. ... .'

Father was singing lustily, enjoying the sound of his own voice, with Mother's sweet soprano blending in. I did my best to keep somewhere in between as unobtrusively as possible, fixing my eyes all the time on Jessie across the way.

There was something different about her head. What was it? A glint of green and blue and deep red.

Suddenly I knew, and felt richer than the laird up in the gallery.

Jessie was wearing my feather in her velour hat.

A Selection of Arrow Bestsellers

☐ Live Flesh	Ruth Rendell	£2.75
☐ Contact	Carl Sagan	£3.50
☐ Yeager	Chuck Yeager	£3.95
☐ The Lilac Bus	Maeve Binchy	£2.50
☐ 500 Mile Walkies	Mark Wallington	£2.50
☐ Staying Off the Beaten Track	Elizabeth Gundrey	£4.95
☐ A Better World Than This	Marie Joseph	£2.95
☐ No Enemy But Time	Evelyn Anthony	£2.95
☐ Rates of Exchange	Malcolm Bradbury	£3.50
☐ For My Brother's Sins	Sheelagh Kelly	£3.50
☐ Carrott Roots	Jasper Carrott	£3.50
☐ Colours Aloft	Alexander Kent	£2.95
☐ Blind Run	Brian Freemantle	£2.50
☐ The Stationmaster's Daughter	Pamela Oldfield	£2.95
☐ Speaker for the Dead	Orson Scott Card	£2.95
☐ Football is a Funny Game	Ian St John and Jimmy Greaves	£3.95
☐ Crowned in a Far Country	Princess Michael of Kent	£4.95

Prices and other details are liable to change

ARROW BOOKS, BOOKSERVICE BY POST, PO BOX 29, DOUGLAS, ISLE OF MAN, BRITISH ISLES

NAME ....

ADDRESS ....

....

....

Please enclose a cheque or postal order made out to Arrow Books Ltd. for the amount due and allow the following for postage and packing.

U.K. CUSTOMERS: Please allow 22p per book to a maximum of £3.00.

B.F.P.O. & EIRE: Please allow 22p per book to a maximum of £3.00.

OVERSEAS CUSTOMERS: Please allow 22p per book.

Whilst every effort is made to keep prices low it is sometimes necessary to increase cover prices at short notice. Arrow Books reserve the right to show new retail prices on covers which may differ from those previously advertised in the text or elsewhere.

Bestselling Fiction

☐ Hiroshima Joe	Martin Booth	£2.95
☐ Voices on the Wind	Evelyn Anthony	£2.50
☐ The Pianoplayers	Anthony Burgess	£2.50
☐ Prizzi's Honour	Richard Condon	£2.95
☐ Queen's Play	Dorothy Dunnett	£3.50
☐ Duncton Wood	William Horwood	£3.50
☐ In Gallant Company	Alexander Kent	£2.50
☐ The Fast Men	Tom McNab	£2.95
☐ A Ship With No Name	Christopher Nicole	£2.95
☐ Contact	Carl Sagan	£3.50
☐ Uncle Mort's North Country	Peter Tinniswood	£2.50
☐ Fletch	Gregory Mcdonald	£1.95
☐ A Better World Than This	Marie Joseph	£2.95
☐ The Lilac Bus	Maeve Binchy	£2.50
☐ The Gooding Girl	Pamela Oldfield	£2.95

Prices and other details are liable to change

ARROW BOOKS, BOOKSERVICE BY POST, PO BOX 29, DOUGLAS, ISLE OF MAN, BRITISH ISLES

NAME ....

ADDRESS ....

....

....

Please enclose a cheque or postal order made out to Arrow Books Ltd. for the amount due and allow the following for postage and packing.

U.K. CUSTOMERS: Please allow 22p per book to a maximum of £3.00.

B.F.P.O. & EIRE: Please allow 22p per book to a maximum of £3.00.

OVERSEAS CUSTOMERS: Please allow 22p per book.

Whilst every effort is made to keep prices low it is sometimes necessary to increase cover prices at short notice. Arrow Books reserve the right to show new retail prices on covers which may differ from those previously advertised in the text or elsewhere.

Bestselling Women's Fiction

☐ Destinies	Charlotte Vale Allen	£2.95
☐ Hester Dark	Emma Blair	£1.95
☐ Nellie Wildchild	Emma Blair	£2.50
☐ Playing the Jack	Mary Brown	£3.50
☐ Twin of Fire	Jude Deveraux	£2.50
☐ Counterfeit Lady	Jude Deveraux	£2.50
☐ Miss Gathercole's Girls	Judy Gardiner	£2.50
☐ A Better World Than This	Marie Joseph	£2.95
☐ Lisa Logan	Marie Joseph	£2.50
☐ Maggie Craig	Marie Joseph	£2.50
☐ For My Brother's Sins	Sheelagh Kelly	£3.50
☐ A Long Way From Heaven	Sheelagh Kelly	£2.95
☐ The Stationmaster's Daughter	Pamela Oldfield	£2.95
☐ The Gooding Girl	Pamela Oldfield	£2.95
☐ The Running Years	Claire Rayner	£2.75
☐ Family Feeling	Judith Saxton	£3.50

Prices and other details are liable to change

ARROW BOOKS, BOOKSERVICE BY POST, PO BOX 29, DOUGLAS, ISLE OF MAN, BRITISH ISLES

NAME ....

ADDRESS ....

....

....

Please enclose a cheque or postal order made out to Arrow Books Ltd. for the amount due and allow the following for postage and packing.

U.K. CUSTOMERS: Please allow 22p per book to a maximum of £3.00.

B.F.P.O. & EIRE: Please allow 22p per book to a maximum of £3.00.

OVERSEAS CUSTOMERS: Please allow 22p per book.

Whilst every effort is made to keep prices low it is sometimes necessary to increase cover prices at short notice. Arrow Books reserve the right to show new retail prices on covers which may differ from those previously advertised in the text or elsewhere.